Exploring
The Ways We Use It

VOCABUREADER
WORKBOOK 4

By

Raymond C. Clark

Illustrated by Robert MacLean

PRO LINGUA **ASSOCIATES**

Published by Pro Lingua Associates
15 Elm Street
Brattleboro, Vermont 05301
802-257-7779
SAN 216-0579

ISBN 0-86647-029-8

This book was set in Century with Century Schoolbook display
type by Stevens Graphics and printed and bound by The Book
Press, both of Brattleboro, Vermont. Designed by Arthur A.
Burrows.

Printed in the United States of America.

Second Printing 1996. 4000 copies in print.

Contents

Special Features

Milestones in the World of Money, page 6 ◆ Wages and Salaries, 17 ◆ Credit Application, 35 ◆ Stock Market Data, 45 ◆ Balance Sheet, 51 ◆ Gambling Entries and Results, 60 ◆ Names of the World's Currencies, 66 ◆ Income Tax Return, 75.

Acknowledgements

I would like to thank the many people who helped me, directly and indirectly, in the writing and preparation of this material. The material was written for intermediate level English language students at the Center for International Banking Studies (CIBS) in Istanbul, Turkey. I would like to acknowledge the support of the staff of the Center and its General Manager, Kenneth P. Pasternak.

Special thanks are due to Aslam Aziz and Lee Sherrill, banking course directors at CIBS. They helped me understand the vocabulary of banking and finance.

The English program at CIBS is a program of The School for International Training, Brattleboro, Vermont. My SIT colleagues in Istanbul were Janie Duncan, Daryl Newton, Kathleen Quinby and Melinda Taplin. Along with them I learned and taught a lot of "Financial English," and I have put some of that knowledge to use in the preparation of this material. A special thank you to Janie Duncan who helped write some of the exercises.

I used this material with my intermediate level class, and their comments were especially helpful. So, many thanks to Talip Akbulut, Arif Bozkurt, Semih Çağlar, Arzu Kara, Nagehan Karaer, Ahmet Kasnaklı, Levent Köroğlu, Sinan Soytutan and Yeşim Tıkıroğlu.

Finally, I am grateful for the assistance of Nazlı Kıral, who also typed the original manuscript, and for the assistance of Andy Burrows and Jon Clark.

Raymond C. Clark
Istanbul, 1988

INTRODUCTION

This book is a vocabulary development text focusing on words associated with the use of money. This special vocabulary is presented in fourteen readings with accompanying exercises. The passages are written in a redundant style so that you can learn the definition of each key word through the context. Although you may have to use a dictionary from time to time, you should try to understand the meaning of the word by studying the sentences and words which precede and follow the key word. In that way, you can develop both new vocabulary and good reading skills. The book is organized according to the following plan:

Reading

Each reading selection describes one aspect of the ways in which people use money. The key vocabulary is in **boldface**.

Exercises

Four exercises follow each reading selection. The exercises progress from easy to more difficult and require you to explore the forms and meanings of the key words. In the fourth exercise, the words are often used in a context that is not about money. The exercises are not tests. They are teaching exercises, and it is expected you will make some mistakes. You can teach yourself by using the answers in the back of the book, but try to do the exercises first, before you check the answers.

Answers

The answers for all the exercises are found at the back of the book.

Key Word Index

This is an alphabetical list of all the key words and the number of the page on which they appear.

An Introductory Reading

Basic human physical **needs** are food, shelter, and clothing, but in today's world we need money to get food, shelter, and clothing. To get money, we **earn** it by making **goods** or providing **services** that are necessary, **useful**, and enjoyable. Some goods, such as food and clothing, are **necessities**; some goods, such as jewelry, are **luxuries**. Services are different from goods; one person does something for another person. Teaching, for example, is a service.

We **use** money every day. We use it in different forms, such as coins, bills, and checks, and we do many different things with our money — buying, saving and borrowing, for example. All of the things we do with money can be called **economic** activity. The science of studying this activity is **economics**. The economic system is called **the economy**, and a person who studies all this is an **economist**.

The organizations at the center of all this activity are banks. We use banks for many purposes, and banks use money for many purposes, but the basic purpose of most banks is to earn money.

Key words

needs	necessity	economic	earns
goods	services	useful	economist
luxury	use	economics	

I. In the following sentences, fill in the blank with one of the key words above. Use each word only once.

1. For most of us, beautiful expensive clothes are a _____, but for all of us, clothes are a _____.

2. Things such as clothes, books and machines are _____, and activities such as teaching, selling goods, and changing money are _____.

3. Most people carry money with them because they need to _____ it every day.

4. Banks provide a _____ service.

5. He teaches _____, and he explains _____ theory. He is an _____.

6. His _____ are very simple: food, fire and friends.

7. She _____ a lot of money by selling clothes.

II. Fill in the blanks with the appropriate word, as in this example:
A person who teaches is a *teacher* .

1. A person who works in a bank is a _____.

2. A person who buys things is a _____.

3. A person who sells things is a _____.

4. A person who uses things is a _____.

5. A person who earns things is an _____.

6. A person who borrows is a _____.

7. But a person who studies economics is an _____.

Money
A Short History

Money, as we know it today, comes in two forms: **coins** and **bills**, also called **currency**. Coins are made from metal, and bills are made from paper. Sometimes bills are called paper money. But, as we shall see later, money also exists in another way in the form of bank deposits.

In earlier days, and even today in some isolated parts of the world, people developed a form of money that was called **commodity** money. This was the use of things that by themselves had some value or importance and could be used as a standard measure of exchange. For example, one cow might be **worth** twenty bags of rice or thirty chickens. Some examples of this kind of money are sea shells in New Guinea, rice in Japan, and iron bars in Nigeria.

Little by little people began to use **precious** metals as a convenient form of commodity money, and gold, silver, and copper eventually became the most commonly used metals. They were useful because they could be carried, they could be split into smaller sizes, and perhaps because of their beauty, they were acceptable as **payment** for something in many different places.

3

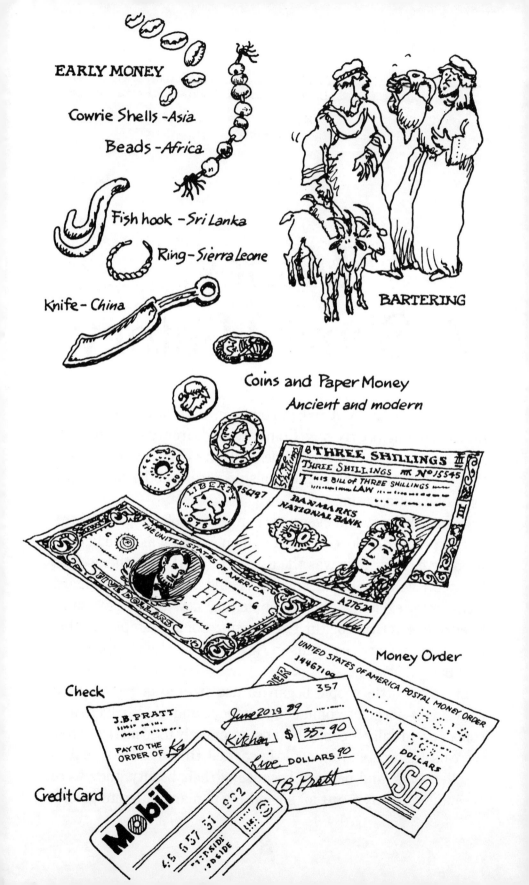

EARLY MONEY

Cowrie Shells – Asia

Beads – Africa

Fish hook – Sri Lanka

Ring – Sierra Leone

Knife – China

BARTERING

Coins and Paper Money
Ancient and modern

8 THREE SHILLINGS
THREE SHILLINGS MR N° 15545
THIS BILL of THREE SHILLINGS LAW

DANMARKS
NATIONAL BANK
50

THE UNITED STATES OF AMERICA
LIBERTY 1976
FIVE DOLLARS FIVE

A2762A

Money Order

Check

UNITED STATES OF AMERICA POSTAL MONEY ORDER
1446710g
357

J.B. PRATT
June 20 19 89
PAY TO THE ORDER OF Ka
Kitchen $ 35.90
five DOLLARS 90
J.B. Pratt

DOLLARS
SA

Credit Card

Mobil
45 6 57 51 002

But there were disadvantages. They could be debased (base metals such as lead and tin could be added to decrease the purity), and it was necessary to weigh the metal each time a **transaction** was made and people exchanged the precious metal for goods or services.

The solution was to **mint** coins from the metal. To show and guarantee the value of the coin, symbols of national authority, such as the head of the king, were stamped on the coins. The use of coinage goes back over 2,500 years, to the Lydians of Anatolia (now Turkey), and the use of coins in international trade goes back at least to the time of Alexander the Great. All of these early coins shared one feature — the **value** of the coin was based on the amount of precious metal that it contained.

During the seventeenth century, bank notes first came into use as currency, the beginning of an important development. At first the bank note was a promise to pay in coin, but the note itself had no actual value. The value of the note was tied to precious metal. This is no longer true, but until early in the twentieth century almost all currencies were tied to gold or silver.

The final step in the development of money was reached in this century when we began to think of bank deposits (the amount we have in our check books and saving books) as the same as the **cash** that we carry in our pockets, purses, and wallets. In fact, in today's world the major part of the world's **supply** of money does not exist as coins and bills but only as numbers on the books of the world's banks. For this reason, it is possible to say that most of the world's money does not exist.

Milestones
in the World of Money

640	B.C.	◆ First true coins developed by Lydians.
560-546	B.C.	◆ Croesus creates the world's first official government coinage.
600's	A.D.	◆ Paper money in use in China.
1100's	A.D.	◆ Development of banks in Italy (The name bank comes from the Latin bancus, "bench.")
1689	A.D.	◆ Lloyd's of London issues the first insurance policy.
1690	A.D.	◆ First paper money in the U.S. issued by Massachusetts Bay Colony.
1694	A.D.	◆ Bank of England established.
1792	A.D.	◆ U.S. dollar and the national mint in Philadelphia established.
1913	A.D.	◆ U.S. Federal Reserve System created.
1929	A.D.	◆ The Great Stock Market Crash.
1944	A.D.	◆ Bretton Woods Conference resulting in establishment of the International Monetary Fund (IMF) and the World Bank.

Key words

coins	commodity	payment	minted
bills	worth	transaction	cash
currency	precious	value	supply

I. Use the key words above in the following sentences. Use each word only once.

1. This coin is not _____ a lot of money. In fact, it is almost worthless.

6

2. In addition to gold and silver, platinum is also a _____ metal

3. _____ are not made out of paper, but _____ are.

4. He never carries _____ with him.

5. Rice is a _____.

6. The _____ of Japan, the yen, has increased in _____ in recent years.

7. The act of buying and selling something can be called a business _____.

8. The company is expecting to receive _____ for its services within 30 days.

9. The government has never _____ a two-dollar coin.

10. Is the world's money _____ constantly increasing?

II. Underline the correct form of the key word.

1. This jewelry is very (value, valued, valuable).

2. That country (supplies, supply, supplying) the world with many valuable (commodities, commodity).

3. (Cash, Cashed, Cashing) a check is a common (transactional, transaction, transacted) at a bank.

4. Tin is not a (preciously, precious) metal.

5. How much is the German mark (worthless, worthwhile, worth)?

6. The (coined, coining, coinage) of the U.S includes pennies, nickels, dimes, quarters, and half-dollars; the common (bill, bills, billings) include the one-, two-, five-, ten-, and twenty-dollar bank notes.

7. The dollar is the basic unit of the (currencies, current, currently) of Canada, Australia, and New Zealand.

8. Will you accept a check in (pay, payment, paying) for these things.

9. The place where coins are (mints, minting, minted) is called a (mint, minter, minting).

7

III. Use the correct form of the key word in parentheses.

1. (value) She has a lot of _____ jewelry. Its
   _____ is probably more than $10,000.

2. (worth) This coin has no value; it is _____.

3. (mint, supply) The U.S. _____ has _____ us with our coins.

4. (commodity) Gold and silver are _____.

5. (payment) They will _____ for their car in monthly
   _____.

6. (transaction) His new company _____ a lot of business in
   the first few days of this month. The very first _____
   involved thousands of pounds.

7. (cash) I needed some _____, so I _____ a check.

IV. Use a key word in these sentences.

1. Can you change a twenty-dollar _____?

2. This coin has just come from the mint; it's in _____
   condition.

3. This land is still _____ a lot of money, but its
   _____ has decreased a little since last year.

4. _____ stones, such as diamonds, can be very expensive.

5. The _____ market includes food, livestock, and metals.

6. They will accept only _____ in _____ for
   their product.

7. In the _____ market people buy and sell _____,
   such as dollars, francs, yen, and marks.

8. You'll need a _____ to use a public vending machine it's
   _____—operated.

9. The act of putting money in a bank can be called a _____.

10. Saudia Arabia is an important _____ of oil. It
    _____ much of the oil consumed in Europe.

8

Using Money

In simple terms we receive money for our work, and we **exchange** this money for things that we need or want. The money comes in to us, and the money goes out to somebody else who then exchanges it for something that he needs, and so on. Money, then, is actually a medium of exchange that enables people to exchange goods and services in a convenient and efficient way. Money is like the oil and grease that we use to keep the great economic machine working.

The most common way in which people get money is to earn it by working, and although we often use the phrase "make money" to mean "earn it," in fact we do not actually mint coins or print bills. Only **counterfeiters** print their own money, illegally.

Let's look at what happens after we are paid for our work. Basically, we have two choices, we can **save** it or **spend** it on something. The decisions that each individual person makes on saving and spending, when taken together with everybody else's decisions, can have a major effect on the economy.

If we decide to save our money, there are several ways in which we can save. We can simply keep our money in a safe place, just as a child may keep coins in a "piggy bank." But money saved in this way can actually lose value if prices rise while the money is sitting in a safe place. Another way to save money is to **invest** it, which means that we let somebody else use the money and they pay us **interest**. In this way, our savings earn money.

If a person prefers or needs to use his money, he probably will buy something, let's say food, from somebody else. The thing that is bought is called a **purchase**. Buying and selling are two very basic activities in the world of business. The businessperson's goal is to make money, just like anybody else who works, but occasionally a businessperson who spends more on his business than he earns will lose money.

Another activity that is familiar to all of us is **borrowing** and **lending**. On a personal level, people often borrow money from each other for a short time (and sometimes forget to repay it). And in the world of business, making **loans** (lending money) is one of the main activities of a bank.

Finally, we should mention two other activities associated with money. Some people like to **collect** money, especially coins, and sometimes a good coin collection can be a good investment. Other people like to **gamble** with their money by buying lottery tickets, going to horse races, or spending time and money in gambling casinos in places like Monaco and Las Vegas.

Key words

exchanges	spent	purchase	lend
counterfeit	investment	borrow	collection
save	interest	loan	gamble

I. Use the key words above in the following sentences. Use each word only once.

1. I ＿＿＿＿＿＿ all my money on clothes, so now I need a ＿＿＿＿＿＿. Can I ＿＿＿＿＿＿ $20.00 from you? If you'll ＿＿＿＿＿＿ me the money, I'll give you＿＿＿＿＿＿.

2. The worker ＿＿＿＿＿＿ his labor for money. He uses it to ＿＿＿＿＿＿ goods. He may ＿＿＿＿＿＿ some of it.

3. I don't think this property is a good ＿＿＿＿＿＿, but if you like to ＿＿＿＿＿＿, you could take a chance. Its value might increase.

4. He thought his coin ＿＿＿＿＿＿ was very valuable, until he discovered that the "Spanish doubloons" were all ＿＿＿＿＿＿ and therefore worthless.

II. Underline the correct form of the key word.

1. How much did you (spend, spending, spent) on food last week?

2. Would you (lend, lending, lent) me some money?

3. A bank makes money by (loans, loaned, loaning) it.

4. Have you ever (borrow, borrowing, borrowed) money from a bank?

5. After she had (saved, saving, saves) a lot of money, she (purchases, purchased, purchase) a new car.

6. My friend (investment, invests, invest) in bonds and makes over $500 a month in (interests, interest, interesting).

7. (Gamble, Gambling, Gambler) is very exciting for the (gamble, gambling, gambler), just as (collecting, collects, collection) money is exciting for the (collection, collector, collecting).

8. (Counterfeits, Counterfeiting, Counterfeiter) is illegal.

9. Workers (exchange, exchanging, exchanges) work for money.

12

III. Use the correct form of the key word in parentheses.

1. (loan) My parents _____ me the money for the new car I bought.

2. (borrow) I also _____ some money from my grandmother.

3. (interest) Naturally, they didn't charge me any _____.

4. (purchase) I actually _____ the car last week.

5. (spend) I _____ some more money on the registration and insurance.

6. (counterfeit) The police finally caught the _____.

7. (collect) Another word for a coin _____ is a numismatist, a person who _____ coins.

8. (gamble, save) I don't like to _____; I would rather put my money into a _____s account.

9. (invest) He _____ all his money in that company, and lost it all.

10. (exchange) The basis of business is the _____ of goods or services for money.

IV. Use a key word in these sentences.

1. I _____ stamps and coins. Would you _____ some stamps for me so I can add them to my _____?

2. Can I _____ this shirt for another one that is smaller?

3. The police caught the _____ as he was trying to _____ his "funny money" at my store.

4. My father is going to _____ in some land. He thinks it will be a good _____. But first, he needs to get a _____ from a bank.

5. Right now, my savings account is paying 5% _____.

6. Drinking alcohol and driving a car is not only against the law. It is _____ with your life.

13

Earning Money

When people work they produce something, and what they produce has value. In today's complex world, it is not always easy to understand how one kind of work has greater value than another kind of work. For example, a farmer produces food, which everyone needs, and a rock star produces music, which is not usually considered a need. But the difference between the **income** of the farmer and the rock star is huge. Of course, there are many reasons why there is such a difference. The farmer's production is somewhat limited, and even though the owner of a large farm may produce enough food to feed several thousand people, a rock star's hit song may be sold on records and tapes to millions of people, and his **royalties** from these sales may amount to millions of dollars. Rock stars can become millionaires. Farmers rarely do.

Another difference between the rock star and the farmer is that the farmer produces goods while the rock musician provides a service. Most of the world's jobs can be classified in this way. In general, complex societies have more people working in services.

Another way in which **employment** can be characterized is by its workforce. In general, "blue-collar" workers work with their hands and are paid hourly **wages**. "White-collar" workers work with their heads and are paid an annual **salary**. However, they are both paid on a regular basis, (weekly, bi-weekly, monthly) usually with a paycheck. Payday, whether weekly or bi-weekly is an important day. In one other way, there is a difference: White-collar employees often have a **contract** with their employer. The contract is an agreement that sometimes protects the employee for certain periods of time and guarantees a certain salary. Blue-collar workers, on the other hand, may not have a personal contract with their employer, but they belong to a union which has a contract with the employer. When it is time for a new contract, the union may ask for a **raise** in pay so that the workers will get more money. Some employers give their employees a **bonus**, a special payment for doing something very well.

Some kinds of professional people, for example doctors and lawyers, receive **fees** for their services. Some experts who work for short periods of time for very specific jobs, such as building a bridge or advising a business or a government, are called **consultants**, and they may receive a one-time payment. Sometimes they are paid a lot of money, and sometimes they are given a small gift called an honorarium.

Then there are a few people who don't need to work because they already have a great deal of **wealth**. Some of them continue to work to earn more, while others have never worked or are retired. In any case, their wealth works for them. They may have their money invested in banks or in the stock market, or they may have their money invested in the ownership of property; both forms of wealth are called **capital**. And this is the origin of the well-known label, capitalist. A capitalist is anyone whose wealth (capital) is invested to earn them more money.

Wages and Salaries

How much money do people in various occupations make per year? It depends on many things: how long they have worked at their job, how skilled they are, how much education they have, whether they are union members, and in many cases unfortunately (even though it is against the law) whether they are male or female. It also depends on how many other people are looking for similar jobs and on where they live. In New York where the cost of living is very high, for example, a carpenter must earn more money than a carpenter with the same qualifications who lives in a smaller town or in the country. Here are the annual wages or salaries of several people who have full-time jobs in a typical small American town.

a fast-food worker	$ 9,724
a store clerk	10,364
a restaurant cook	11,874
a waitress	12,378
a licensed practical nurse	17,365
a meat cutter	19,516
an administrative assistant	20,529
an office manager	21,415
a retail store manager	22,285
an electrical technician	22,719
a teacher	23,806
a physical therapist	25,099
a computer programmer	26,623
an accountant	29,263
a bank manager	30,104
a business manager	36,104
a systems analyst	36,515

Key words

income	wages	fee	consultant
royalties	salary	raise	wealthy
employed	contract	bonus	capital

I. Use the key words above in the following sentences. Use each word only once.

1. The singer's income from _____ is more than $500,000 a year. He must be a millionaire by now.
2. The workers want a new _____ with the owners.
3. The lawyer's _____ for his services is $500.
4. The employees' daily _____ have not increased.
5. She is paid an annual _____; her _____ is over $30,000 a year.
6. Any business needs _____ in order to operate.
7. As a _____, he earned an honorarium of $3,000 for his services.
8. I'm not _____; I don't have a lot of money.
9. She has been _____ by that company for ten years.
10. I've got to ask for a _____; I'm not making enough money.
11. On January 1, all the employees got a New Year's _____ because the company did very well during the previous year.

II. Underline the correct form of the key word.

1. "You're a (capital, capitalist, capitalistic)," he shouted.
2. The royal family is extremely (wealth, wealthy).
3. The athlete has refused to sign a (contract, contracted, contractual) with his team.
4. Their expenses are greater than their (income, incoming).
5. She collects (royalty, royalties, royal) checks from several different recording companies.
6. Although prices have gone up, (wage, waged, wages) have not.
7. The company gave all its (employer, employees, employment) a (salary, salaried, salaries) increase.
8. All his earnings this year came from (fee, fees, feed).

18

9. Let's (consulting, consult, consultant) with an expert on this problem.
10. Not all of the employees got (raise, raised, raises) this year.
11. Only a few people got (bonus, bonuses) _____ this year.

III. Use the correct form of the key word in parentheses.

1. (salary) The cost of living has gone up, but our _____ haven't.
2. (wage) The minimum _____ is $4.50 an hour.
3. (wealth, income) Although he is extremely _____, he didn't pay any _____ tax last year.
4. (consult) We need an expert. Let's get a _____.
5. (employ) After three months of unemployment he was happy to be _____ again.
6. (royalty) She gets a 20% _____ on all her books.
7. (bonus, raise) Both of them got _____ and _____.
8. (fee) Yes, he's a good doctor, but his _____ are very high.
9. (capital) We have studied socialism and _____.

IV Use a key word in these sentences.

1. Her company _____ over 500 people.
2. Real _____ is the actual property of a business, except its cash.
3. The managers all got a 10% _____ increase.
4. The hourly _____ rate is $5.50.
5. His wife still receives the _____ from the book he wrote.
6. As a highly paid _____, he needs to work only a few months each year.
7. The bank will charge a small _____ for this service.
8. The union is asking for a 10% pay _____.
9. The football player signed a _____ with the Giants.
10. Most states have a state _____ tax.
11. Early to bed and early to rise keeps one healthy, _____, and wise.
12. Something extra that we don't expect to receive is a _____.

19

Buying and Selling

Most of us use currency when we are in the act of buying or selling something, although more and more people use checks and credit cards. Buying and selling is the basis for the world of business. A simple description of business is the **production**, **distribution** and sale of goods and services for a **profit**. In other words, business is based on selling the product at a price that is higher than the cost of making and delivering the product or goods.

There are two kinds of sales: **wholesale** and **retail**. In wholesale trade, a producer sells large quantities of his product to a retailer (a store owner, for example) and the retailer sells the product in small amounts to individual **consumers**. In the auto industry, for example, the manufacturer of the car sells it wholesale to a retailer (called a **dealer** in the auto industry) who in turn charges a higher price and sells the car to a customer. Both the wholesaler and the retailer hope to make a profit from their transactions.

A very important part of contemporary business is **marketing**. Marketing is important because businesses are in **competition** with each other to sell their products to customers. It is obvious that it is important to get and maintain a market share that will allow a company to be competitive and make a profit. Marketing influences the entire business cycle from production to sales, and in recent years the **promotion** of the product, especially in advertisements, has become a very important operation.

In the final act, when buyer and seller are face to face, most sales are based on a fixed price. However, some transactions, especially those for very expensive items such as houses and automobiles are done through **bargaining**, in which the buyer can make an **offer** that is below the asking price. Sometimes in private sales, where an individual might be selling a used refrigerator, the buyer and seller may also bargain.

In another kind of sales transaction, especially when a government is purchasing goods or services, the buyer asks for competitive **bids** and several suppliers each make a bid for a contract to supply the goods or services. The lowest bidder, of course, gets the contract. In a somewhat similar situation, a person or entity may sell something by auction. In an auction, the seller asks the buyer to make a bid, and the highest bid gets the product, as the auctioneer says "going, going, gone!" which means the sale is completed.

Key words

production	wholesale	dealer	promotion	bid
distribution	retail	marketing	bargain	
profit	consumer	competitors	offer	

I.   Use the key words above in the following sentences. Use each word only once.

1. Consumers have not been spending; therefore ＿＿＿＿＿＿＿ sales are down.

2. A _____ buys cars at _____ and sells them to
   a _____ at retail.
3. We need to make a 20% _____ if we're going to stay in
   business, but our _____ are selling their product at a
   very low price.
4. Machines are used in the _____ of goods.
   Vehicles are used in the _____ of goods.
   Advertisements are used in the _____ of products.
5. The price is $5,000, but I'm going to _____ $4,500.
6. At an auction, the highest _____ wins.
7. Our new _____ manager wants to change the name of
   our product and advertise it on TV.
8. If you buy something at a very low price, you can say you got a

   _____.

II. Give the correct form of the word. Be sure to check your answers for
   the correct spelling.

   1. A person who consumes is a _____.
   2. A person who bids is a _____. (Watch the spelling!)
   3. A person who deals is a _____.
   4. A person in distribution is a _____.
   5. A person in promotion is a _____.
   6. A person who makes an offer is an _____.
   7. A person in production is a _____.
   8. A person in wholesale trade is a _____.
   9. A person in retail trade is a _____.
   10. A person involved in _____ is a competitor.
   11. A person who makes a very high _____ can be called a
      profiteer.

III. Underline the correct form of the key word.

   1. What a (deal, dealt, dealing)! I bought the refrigerator at almost
      wholesale, wholesaling), and I didn't even (bargaining, bargain,
      bargained).

23

2. In order to (market, marketing, marketable) our product in Tokyo, we need to (promotion, promote, promoter) it on TV.

3. Their new (production, product, producer) is priced way below ours. How can we (competitive, competition, compete) with them?

4. The government report says that retail (consumers, consume, consumption) has increased in the last few months. This has made (retailers, retailing, retail) very happy. Their (profiting, profiteers, profits) will be higher.

5. We have a new (distribution, distributor) for the West Coast market.

6. That's a beautiful chair. Let's make an (offering, offer). Shall we (bid, bidding) $25?

IV. Use a key word in these sentences.

1. How much will you _____ me for this Persian carpet?

2. When you're in Boston, be sure to visit Quincy _____; it's a great place to shop.

3. General Motors has _____ millions of automobiles.

4. Athletes from all over the world will be _____ in the Olympics.

5. They under- _____ us and got the contract.

6. We can say that a person who learns from his mistakes, _____ from them.

7. The average _____ buys twenty-four bars of soap every year.

8. In a card game, the person who takes and gives the cards is called the _____.

9. The post office is involved in the _____ of mail.

10. She spent two days _____ for the car, and finally bought it for $2,500. I think she got a good _____.

11. Advertising is one form of _____. The verb to _____ can also mean "to give a higher position." For example, he was _____ to Vice President.

Banks

For most of us, the most important and best-known **financial** institution is our local bank. Probably our bank is a **commercial** bank, meaning that the bank is involved in **trade**, and what it trades in is money and other financial services. It carries out this trade for a profit, just as any business does.

Banks carry out a variety of functions. For its customers it operates savings and checking accounts; it offers loans; it changes money. With the familiar savings account, the customer can save money and earn interest. The customer **deposits** and **withdraws** money, and his deposits and withdrawals along with his interest earnings and the **balance** (the total of deposits minus withdrawals) are recorded in a passbook.

A checking account is a service that usually makes our lives a little easier. The bank holds our money and we pay our bills with our checks by **drawing** on our accounts. The checks come back to our bank through a clearinghouse and our accounts are charged for the checks we have written. At the end of each month we receive a **statement** which summarizes our transactions. Although checking accounts are very helpful, we can sometimes make problems for ourselves by **bouncing** a check. The check bounces back to us like a ball (a check that bounces is called a rubber check). It is marked insufficient **funds**, meaning we do not have enough money in our account to cover the check; we have overdrawn our account.

25

Banks usually have a service charge for maintaining our checking accounts, although some banks do not charge us if we keep a **minimum** balance in our account. So for example, if the minimum is $500 and our balance never goes below $500, we do not pay a service charge.

In addition to operating accounts, banks also loan money and charge interest on the loans. Although banks always try to keep a certain amount of money in **reserve** to cover withdrawals, they invest a large part of the money they are holding to earn more money. They also offer other services for a fee, such as storing valuables for people in safe deposit boxes inside the bank's vault, changing currencies, and selling traveler's checks.

In short, banks provide services and use our money to make money.

Key words

financial	deposit	draw	funds
commercial	withdraw	statement	minimum
trade	balance	bounced	reserve

I. Use the key words above in the sentences below. Use each key word only once.

1. I'm trying to save money so I ＿＿＿＿＿＿＿ $20 a week in my savings account.

2. I need some money so I'll ＿＿＿＿＿＿＿ $20 from my account.

3. I'm not going to use all my money right now so I'll keep some in

＿＿＿＿＿＿＿.

4. I want to ＿＿＿＿＿＿＿ a check on my account in the First National Bank.

5. I received my bank ＿＿＿＿＿＿＿ this week and it shows that I have a ＿＿＿＿＿＿＿ of $525. That's only $25 above the ＿＿＿＿＿＿＿ balance for the special checking account.

6. A sum or supply of money can be called ＿＿＿＿＿＿＿.

7. Another word for exchange is ＿＿＿＿＿＿＿.

8. A _____ bank hopes to make a profit.

9. The _____ Times is a newspaper that is read by economists, bankers, and business people.

10. He wrote me a bad check; it _____

II. Underline the correct form of the key word.

1. Did you (bounce, bounced, bouncing) a check this month?

2. We don't have enough (fund, funds, funded) in our account.

3. Wall Street is the (financing, financial, financed) center of the U.S.

4. The bank is required to keep a certain amount of money in (reservation, reserving, reserve).

5. We can get 5½% interest if our (balancing, balance, balanced) is above the (minimum, minimal).

6. This month my (deposit, deposits, depositing) were greater than my (withdraws, withdrawals).

7. (Commerce, Commercials) is another word for trade.

8. She works on the stock exchange as a (trade, trading, trader). She probably (draws, draw, drawing) a large salary.

III. Use the correct form of the key word in parentheses.

1. (reserve) Our cash _____ are getting low.

2. (deposit) She _____ the check yesterday,

3. (withdraw) and then she made a _____.

4. (balance) Then she _____ her checkbook.

5. (minimum) and discovered that her balance was below the

_____.

6. (statement) There will be a service charge on her next

_____.

7. (draw) A bank draft is used to _____ on an account.

8. (fund) The World Bank _____ development in Third World countries.

9. (Trade) The tallest buildings in New York are the towers of the World _____ Center.

10. (finance) He was a _____ success at the age of thirty-two.

11. (commerce) The _____ center of the city is near the river.

12. (bounce) Until yesterday, she had never _____ a check.

IV. Use a key word in these sentences.

1. The opposite of maximum is _____.

2. Rubber balls and rubber checks can _____.

3. She _____ her letter in the mail box.

4. The International Monetary _____ (IMF) gives loans to countries.

5. I _____ my objection; everything's OK now.

6. I'm going to _____ out all my savings and buy a car.

7. The company distributed its _____ statement showing its assets, liabilities, and income.

8. The President is going to make a _____ which will describe her position.

9. He's not in the regular army; he's in the _____, which would be used only in an emergency.

10. He has a _____ pilot's license. His business is flying planes.

11. Stamp collectors like to _____ stamps with each other.

Borrowing and Lending

At some time or another almost everybody has said, "I'm **broke**. Can you lend me some money?" On a personal level, a loan may only involve two friends who borrow from and lend to each other to help each other. The person who borrows the money **owes** money to the lender. Occasionally the borrower may sign a very simple agreement called an I.O.U. The borrower **repays** the loan when he can, and usually between friends there is no interest charge.

There are times, however, when people need to borrow a large **sum** of money. For example, buying a car requires a large amount of money, and for that we need an auto loan. The interest rate on these kinds of loans is usually rather high, and they are usually for a **term** of not more than a few years.

Another major purchase is a house, and in the United States banks loan money to people for this. This kind of loan is spread over many years (twenty to thirty years is typical), and it is called a **mortgage**. The bank holds the **deed**, the legal document that proves ownership, until the mortgage is paid off. The home serves as collateral: If the borrower fails to repay the loan, the bank repossesses the house. A family celebration called burning the mortgage takes place when all the money, interest and **principal**, is finally paid off, and the family at last **owns** its own home.

In addition to making loans to individuals, banks also make loans to businesses. From time to time a business needs to borrow money, and thus go into **debt**, to expand the business. If the business seems to be a good **risk**, the bank will extend **credit** to the business, allowing it to borrow up to a certain amount. The bank becomes the creditor, and the business becomes the debtor.

Countries too sometimes need to borrow money, and in the world of international finance, commercial banks often make loans to developing countries. The World Bank, an international development bank, provides special support for long term development projects. In recent years, however, more and more countries have **defaulted** on their loans, and the list of debtor nations gets longer and longer. But it is not only the poor who are in debt. In the United States, Americans have consumed large quantities of foreign goods, but they have not sold as many goods to foreigners. The result is that the United States owes a lot of money to other countries.

With so many people in debt, who are the world's creditors?

Key words

broke	sum	mortgage	debt
owe	term	principal	risk
repay	deed	own	credit
			default

I.   Use the key words above in the following sentences. Use each key word only once.

   1. A period of time can be called a _____.

   2. To have no money is to be _____.

   3. A piece of paper that specifies the owner of a piece of property is a

   _____.

   4. If I borrow money from you, I _____ you money.

5. This house is mine. I ＿＿＿＿＿＿ it.

6. If I owe money, I am in ＿＿＿＿＿＿.

7. If I can't pay back my loan, I am in ＿＿＿＿＿＿.

8. Another word for "pay back" is ＿＿＿＿＿＿.

9. A strong, solid business is a good ＿＿＿＿＿＿.

10. If I give you a loan, I extend ＿＿＿＿＿＿ to you.

11. The original amount of a loan (excluding interest) is the ＿＿＿＿＿＿. If it is a long-term loan for property, it is a ＿＿＿＿＿＿.

12. Another word for "amount" is ＿＿＿＿＿＿

II. Underline the correct form of the key word.

1. Last year I (owe, owed, owing) the bank a lot of money, but I finally (repaid, repay, repayment) it. Now I'm broke again.

2. Mr. Jones, the (term, termination, terminal) of your (mortgaged, mortgage) will be twenty years. The (principality, principle, principal) is $80,000 and the interest is 12%. Keep up the (pay, payments) and the (deed, deeded, deeds) will be yours and you'll (owe, own , owner) the house.

3. Because they (default, defaulted) on their previous loan, they are not a good (risky, risk). Therefore, we can't extend (credits, credit, credited) to them.

4. She had never been a (debt, debtor) before, but she needed a large (summary, sum, sums) of money, so she took out a loan.

33

III. Use the correct form of the key word in parantheses.

1. (repay) I _____ that loan a year ago.
2. (owe) How much do I _____ you?
3. (deed) My _____ is registered with the registrar of _____.
4. (broke) "I can't go; I'm _____," he said.
5. (debt) Although his income is up, so are his _____.
6. (term) Do you need a long-_____ loan?
7. (mortgage) All of this property is _____.
8. (own) The _____ of the house is really the bank.
9. (sum) The monthly payment will be the _____ of the principal plus the interest.
10. (risk) The two partners _____ a lot of their own capital when they started the business.
11. (credit) When their business failed, their _____ took all the property and the inventory.
12. (default) Because its currency has lost 50% of its value, New Naciona has _____ on its loan from World Bank.

IV. Use a key word in these sentences.

1. No I won't lend you any more money. You already _____ me $15, and I'm almost _____ myself. When you've _____ me we can discuss another loan.
2. At last! We've paid off the _____, and the _____ to the house is ours. We _____ our own home.
3. We needed a short- _____ loan, but the bank turned us down.
4. How can I ever repay my _____ to you? You _____ everything you owned to help me.
5. You've asked for a rather large _____ of money, and the maximum amount of _____ we can give you is only $5,000.
6. They have _____ on both the _____ and the interest.

34

IRONTOWN SAVINGS & LOAN
Serving Local Needs Since 1832

CREDIT APPLICATION

DATE	OFFICE	INTERVIEWER	☐ Individual — Complete Sections A&B ☐ Secured — Complete Appropriate Section C

Type of Loan: ☐ Auto ☐ Home Improvement ☐ Personal _____ (Purpose)	Amount of Loan $	No. of Pmts.	Rate	Amt. of Mo. Pmt. $

Joint or Co-Borrower filling out separate application form. Name   Date

SECTION A — INFORMATION REGARDING APPLICANT

Full Name (Last, First, Middle Initial) _____   Birthdate _____

Present Street Address _____   Years there _____

City _____ State _____ Zip _____ Telephone _____

Social Security No. _____

Present Employer _____ Years there _____ Telephone _____

Position or title _____ Name of supervisor _____

Employer's Address _____

Present gross income: per year $ _____ , per month $ _____ No. Dependants _____ Ages _____

Other income $_____ per _____ Source(s) of other income _____

Is any income listed in this section likely to be reduced before the credit requested is paid off?

☐ Yes (Explain in detail on separate sheet)   ☐ No

Checking Account with: _____ Approximate balance: _____

Savings Account with: _____ Approximate balance: _____

Name of nearest relative not living with you _____ Telephone _____

Relationship _____ Address _____

SECTION B — DEBT INFORMATION   This section must be completed by all parties involved in this transaction.

Are you a co-maker, endorser, or guarantor on any loan or contract? No ☐   Yes ☐ Explain:

Are there any unsatisfied judgments against you? No ☐   Yes ☐ If "Yes," Amount $ to whom owed:

Have you been declared bankrupt in the last 14 years? No ☐   Yes ☐ If "Yes," Where?   Year

Other obligations — (E.g., liability to pay alimony, child support, separate maintenance, Use separate sheet if necessary).

RESIDENCE — RENTER Landlord's Name   Landlord's Address   Landlord's Tel. No.   Monthly Pmt. $

RESIDENCE — HOME OWNER Mtg. Holder (if paid, past Mtg. Holder Name)   Account Number

Orig. Pur. Price $ Pres. Mkt. Value $ Monthly Pymt. $ Address   Orig. Mtg. Balance $ Current Balance $

OUTSTANDING OBLIGATIONS: On a separate sheet of paper, list ALL other open loans/charge accounts (debts) or obligations including but not limited to court order(s), and the name in which the account stands if different. Also, list ALL obligations of which you are Co-Maker.

SECTION C — SECURED CREDIT (Complete only if credit is to be secured.)

Motor Vehicle Owned _____ To Purchase _____	FOR HOME IMPROVEMENT LOAN

New or Used	Year	Make and Model	Contractor _____

Sales Price $ _____ Down Payment $ _____	Vehicle Ident. Number	Work to be done _____

Purchased From _____

Address _____   Estimated Costs: _____   Estimates or bids attached ☐

Insured by _____

Address _____

FOR LOANS SECURED BY OTHER ASSETS

In what name will the vehicle be registered? _____   On a separate sheet, identify savings account(s) or other collateral to be pledged.

SECTION E — ALL APPLICANTS MUST SIGN HERE
Everything that I have stated in this application is correct to the best of my knowledge.

Applicant's Signature   Date

35

Plastic Money

"Will this be cash or **charge**?" In many stores today this is the question a **sales** clerk asks a customer as the customer prepares to pay for what he has purchased. The response, "I'll charge it," means that the customer will pay not with currency or with a check but with a charge card, which is sometimes called plastic money. The more common name for the card is, of course, the credit card. Stores and restaurants everywhere often display signs to show that they **accept** credit cards.

It can be dangerous to lose your credit card or have it **stolen** by a thief. And because it is so easy to charge purchases, some people buy more things than they should. But credit cards also carry a credit **limit**, meaning there is a maximum **amount** a person may charge. Credit limits are determined by the credit card company. The company decides on a credit **rating** for each card carrier. A person can get a high rating if he is a good risk, and the higher the rating, the more a person can charge.

Credit cards have become very valuable for travelers, and in many cases even a necessity. Nowadays, it is almost impossible to **rent** a car without a credit card. There is one well-known advertisement on TV for a credit card which says, "Don't leave home without it."

Many stores offer their own charge accounts which enable a customer to charge purchases at that store only. Some places allow people to buy things on time, meaning that the customer can make a **down payment** for part of the total **cost**, and than pay the balance later in regular payments or **installments**. This is called an installment plan. Often there is an additional-charge for this service, which is called the finance charge.

Many banks now issue a plastic card that can be used with automatic teller machines so that the customer can do his banking after hours and on weekends. In some cases this card can be used in stores, and through a process called electronic funds **transfer** (EFT), the money is automatically moved from the customer's bank account to the store's account. The transfer is done electronically by a computer, and this process is much faster than the traditional charge card. Maybe some time in the future paper money will no longer be used for buying and selling.

Key words

charge	stolen	rating	cost
sales	limit	rent	installments
accept	amount	down payment	transfer

I. Use one of the key words above in the following sentences. Use each key word only once.

1. They _____ all major credit cards at that hotel.
2. You'll need a credit card if you're going to _____ a car.
3. I want to _____ $500 from my checking account to my savings account.
4. The total _____ of this refrigerator is $700. But if you make a _____ _____ of $100, your monthly _____ will be only $50, plus a small finance charge.
5. I can't find my purse. I think it was _____. Fortunately, I was carrying only a small _____ of cash.
6. I don't understand why you won't let me _____ this purchase. My credit _____ is excellent, and on my credit card I have a _____ of $1,000.
7. It has not been a good month. Our _____ have been down by 50%.

II. Underline the correct form of the key word in parentheses.

1. It's gone! Somebody (steal, stole, stolen) my car.
2. I'd like to open a (charge, charged, charging) account.
3. Will you (accept, accepted, accepting) my traveler's check?
4. In order to increase our (sale, sales), we are having a big end-of-the-year sale. We hope to sell almost everything.
5. He's so rich his credit is (limit, limited, unlimited).
6. How much does this (cost, costs, costing)?
7. Last year she (rent, rented, renting) an apartment near the university.
8. All of my charges last month (amount, amounted, amounting) to only £85.

39

9. We closed our savings account and (transfer, transferred, transferring) all our funds to a special account.

10. If you don't pay your bills, you won't get a good credit (rate, rating).

III. Use the correct form of the key word in parentheses.

1. (rent) How much is the ＿＿＿＿＿＿＿＿ on this apartment?

2. (accept) We are pleased to announce that we are now ＿＿＿＿＿＿＿＿ all major credit cards.

3. (installment) She has only paid three ＿＿＿＿＿＿＿＿.

4. (transfer) I have ＿＿＿＿＿＿＿＿ all my money to another account.

5. (cost) The ＿＿＿＿＿＿＿＿ of consumer goods is increasing.

6. (steal) Somebody has been in our room, but I don't think anything was ＿＿＿＿＿＿＿＿.

7. (charge) Let's ＿＿＿＿＿＿＿＿ it, instead of paying cash.

8. (Sale) There is a "For ＿＿＿＿＿＿＿＿" sign on their house.

9 (limit) There is no ＿＿＿＿＿＿＿＿ to the number of transactions you can make on this account.

10. (amount) They stole a huge ＿＿＿＿＿＿＿＿ of money.

11. (payment) The monthly ＿＿＿＿＿＿＿＿ are only $35.

IV. Use a key word in these sentences.

1. I'm going to ＿＿＿＿＿＿＿＿ to another university.

2. They put all their savings into a ＿＿＿＿＿＿＿＿ on a house.

3. Please ＿＿＿＿＿＿＿＿ my apology.

4. His business lost a rather large ＿＿＿＿＿＿＿＿ of money last year.

5. There is a ＿＿＿＿＿＿＿＿ to the amount we can spend for rent.

6. The ＿＿＿＿＿＿＿＿ clerk forgot to give me my change.

7. When the police finally caught them, they had sold all the ＿＿＿＿＿＿＿＿ works of art.

8. I don't want to pay now; I'll ＿＿＿＿＿＿＿＿ it.

9. He is ＿＿＿＿＿＿＿＿ a room at the hotel that ＿＿＿＿＿＿＿＿ $95 a night. The hotel has a five-star ＿＿＿＿＿＿＿＿.

10. On our new ＿＿＿＿＿＿＿＿ plan, all you need is $10 down.

Investing

Investing money means saving money so that the value of the money invested will increase and the money will produce income or profit.

Savings accounts and time deposits (withdrawals are possible only after a specified period of time) are well-known ways of investing money. Another way of investing is to buy **securities**. Stocks and bonds are two kinds of securities that people invest in. A stock, in other terms, means a **share** in some business; so people who buy stocks, actually become owners of part of the business — shareholders.

There are two kinds of stocks: common and preferred, and a basic difference between them is that a preferred stock is a **safer** investment, but it is more **expensive** than the lower-**priced** (**cheaper**) common stock.

Why do people invest in stocks? One reason is that stock in a successful company can pay **dividends** (a share of the profit) that are higher than the interest on a savings account. If the company is successful, the value of the share can also increase and the owner of the share can sell it for a high price, and thereby make a profit, which is called a capital **gain**. Of course, the stock market can be risky because some businesses may not do well, and the investor may lose money. In a way, investing in stocks

41

can be like gambling, and for that reason many people rely on a **broker** to advise them and manage their investments by buying and selling securities for them.

Probably the most famous stock exchange is Wall Street in New York City where millions of shares are traded every day. People with investments follow the stock market reports closely to watch how their stocks are going. When the general **trend** of the market is up, the market is described as "bullish," and when it is down, it is "bearish."

Another form of investment is bonds. A bond is **issued** by a government or a company to raise money. A bond is essentially a loan, and a bondholder does not become an owner of the company, like a shareholder. Although the **yield** on bonds is generally lower than that on good stocks, bonds are usually considered safer.

There are many other ways to invest money. Land and buildings (real estate) can be a good investment. Collectibles, such as rare and valuable coins and stamps or works of art are sometimes good investments. In the United States one unusual kind of collectible is the baseball card — small pictures of baseball players that children buy. A 1952 card of the famous baseball player Mickey Mantle is worth $4,810. Purchased for about one cent ($0.01), that is an increase of 481,000 per cent — a pretty good yield.

Key words

securities	expensive	price	trend
shares	cheap	gain	issues
safe	dividend	broker	yield

I. Use one of the key words above in the sentences below. Use each key word only once.

1. This computer is very _____, but the more _____ one is a better buy because it can do more.

43

2. I bought that stock when the _____ was $47.00 and sold it recently for $87.00. My _____ was $40.00.

3. Stocks and bonds are _____. Another word for secure is _____.

4. I'm going to call my _____ and have her sell all my _____ in that company.

5. This bond will _____ 5%.

6. She received a very nice _____ this year from her ABM stock.

7. This is a listing of all the new bond _____.

8. Recently, the market _____ has been bullish.

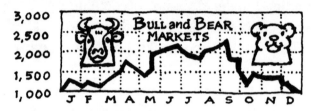

II. Underline the correct form of the key word.

1. Our company did not pay a (dividend, dividends) this year.

2. In today's trading there were more losers than (gains, gainers, gained).

3. A (broke, broker) must carefully study the (trending, trend, trended) of the market.

4. If the (prices, priced, price) is right, I'll buy.

5. A "blue chip" stock is usually one of the most (expensiver, expensive, expense) ones.

6. Wholesale prices are (more cheap, cheapest, cheaper) than retail prices.

7. Last year they (issue, issues, issued) several thousand new stocks. They were a good investment; they (yield, yielded, yielding) almost $50 a share in dividends.

8. A deed for a house can be given as a (security, securities, secure) for a loan.

9. These (share, sharing, shares) are a (safest, safe, safety) investment.

44

NYSE

New York Stock Exchange

52 Weeks High	Low	Stock	Div.	Yld %	P-E Ratio	Sales 100s	High	Low	Close	Net Chg.
— A — A — A —										
72⅞	40	ASA	3.00	7.8	...	492	40¾	40⅛	40⅝	+ ½
23⅞	12¼	AlskAir	.16	.9	14	415	17⅞	17⅝	+ ⅛	
64¾	33¾	Alcoa	1.40	2.7	8	1481	51¼	50½	51⅛	+ ¼
60	36½	AmBrnd	2.20	4.7	9	1081	47¼	46	47⅛	+ 1⅛
39⅞	20¾	AmExp	.76	2.8	21	5177	27⅛	26⅜	27⅛	+ ⅝
35⅞	23	AT&T	1.20	4.6	14	15652	26½	26	26¼	+ ⅛
14¾	7⅛	Armco		...	23	2233	11⅛	10⅞	11⅛	+ ¼
99⅛	58¾	AtlRich	4.00	4.9	10	2184	81½	80⅜	81	+ ⅝
38⅝	19¼	Avon	2.00	8.2	12	1233	24⅞	24⅜	24½	+ ⅜
— B — B — B —										
46⅞	25⅝	Ball	1.08	3.8	11	506	28⅝	27⅞	28⅝	+ ⅝
35⅞	17⅞	BkBost	1.08	3.9	10	1049	27⅝	27¼	27½	...
14⅝	6⅝	BnkAm		...	9	2663	13⅝	13⅜	13⅝	+ ⅛
26½	13	BlackD	.40	1.8	15	2058	21⅞	21¼	21⅞	+ ¼
63⅞	31¼	Borden	1.56	3.0	13	702	51⅝	50⅛	51⅝	+ 1⅜
— C — C — C —										
226¼	140½	CBS	3.00	1.9	15	876	157⅜	157	157⅜	+ ⅜
35⅞	18½	CalFed	1.40	5.8	4	867	24¼	24	24¼	- ¼
46¼	19⅜	Chase	2.16	7.5	3	928	28¾	28½	28¾	+ ⅛
62¾	32	Chevrn	2.60	5.6	11	3779	46⅝	45⅞	46½	+ ⅝
48	19⅝	Chryslr	1.00	4.4	4	7503	22¾	22¼	22⅝	+ ¼
70	50⅞	Chubb	2.16	4.0	7	3449	54¼	53⅜	54¼	+ 1⅜
34¾	17½	Circus s		...	16	328	30¼	30	30⅛	+ 1⅛
52⅝	28	ColgPal	1.48	3.4	40	2257	43	41⅜	43	+ 1⅜
78½	34	Compaq		...	12	10081	59⅞	57	57	- 1¼
— D — D — D —										
60¼	32	DeltaAr	1.20	2.4	9	2415	51¼	50	50⅜	- ⅜
82½	41¼	Disney	.40	.6	18	3532	62¼	60⅞	61¾	+ ⅞
55	26¾	DowJns	.68	2.0	13	386	33½	32¾	33¼	+ ¼
131	75	duPont	3.80	4.5	10	6917	85½	84⅛	84⅞	- ⅛
— E — E — E —										
70⅝	39¾	EKodk s	1.80	4.0	12	10886	44¾	43⅜	44⅝	+ 1⅜
16½	6½	EnvSys		...	29	29	11⅛	11⅛	11⅛	...
50¾	33¼	Exxon s	2.20	4.8	12	9447	46½	45¾	46⅛	+ ½
— F — F — F —										
15½	7⅞	Fairchd	.20	1.9	...	508	10⅜	10⅛	10⅜	+ ⅛
12	4⅜	Fairfd		...	...	113	6⅛	5⅞	6	...
25	⅜	FtRepA		...	...	1977	13/16	½	½	- ⅜
14¾	5¾	Foodmk		...	8	112	12¼	12	12	...
— G — G — G —										
69½	31¾	GAF	.10	.2	13	1367	46¼	45⅛	46⅛	+ ⅝
44¾	29⅜	GTE	2.52	6.4	12	5611	39¾	38⅞	39¼	+ ¼
66⅜	38⅜	GenEl	1.40	3.3	12	13024	42¼	40⅝	41⅞	+ 1¼
21	12¼	Getty s	.20	1.1	9	40	18⅜	18⅛	18⅛	- ⅛
25⅛	13¼	GIANT		...	14	4	16⅜	16¼	16⅜	- ⅛
42⅞	19¼	Greyh	1.32	4.2	125	1371	31¾	31⅛	31¼	- ¾
46¾	29¾	GlfWst s	.70	1.7	15	1165	42¾	41¼	42⅜	+ ⅝
— H — H — H —										
51¾	33½	Heinz	1.24	3.0	14	1834	41	40¼	40¾	+ ½
37¾	20¾	Hrshey	.62	2.6	14	1351	24⅛	23⅝	24	+ ⅜
50⅞	27½	Hilton s	1.00	2.2	15	686	46	44⅝	45⅞	+ ⅞
62½	32½	HousInt	2.14	3.8	10	536	56⅞	55¾	56⅞	+ 1⅜
29½	16½	Human	.92	3.8	11	1580	25	24¼	24½	...
— I — I — I —										
27	16½	IllPowr	2.64	14.2	8	1515	18¾	18½	18⅝	- ⅛
175⅞	100	IBM	4.40	3.6	14	12119	123⅞	121¼	123¾	+ 2⅝
15⅞	1⅞	IT Crp		...	...	2050	3⅜	3¼	3⅜	...
79	37¾	IrvBnk	2.42	3.6	9	478	67⅞	67½	67½	- ⅜
— J — J — J —										
17⅝	6¾	Jackpot	.24b	1.5	18	247	16⅛	15¾	15⅞	- ⅛
14⅞	5⅞	Jamswy	.08	.7	14	786	10¾	10¼	10¾	+ ⅛
105⅜	55	JohnJn	2.00	2.6	14	4651	77½	76	77¼	+ 1
— M — M — M —										
9¾	5½	McDld	.20a	3.0	11	142	6¾	6⅝	6¾	+ ⅛
83½	45	MMM	2.12	3.4	14	5197	62⅞	61½	62¾	+ ¾
55	32	Mobil	2.40	5.4	11	5435	44¼	43½	44⅛	+ ⅜
100¼	57	Monsan	3.00	3.5	11	1114	86⅝	85⅞	86⅜	+ ½
74	35	Motorla	.64	1.4	15	6607	46⅞	45¼	46¼	+ 1
130	99	Marshall	6.60	5.4	19	2903	125	119½	123¾	+ ½
— N — N — N —										
87¼	42	NCR	1.24	2.1	11	3859	58¼	56½	57¾	+ 1⅜
14½	5	Nortek	.10a	1.3	...	48	7⅝	7½	7½	...
21¾	14½	NEurO	1.60e	10.9	9	55	14⅝	14½	14⅝	+ ⅛
51⅛	24¾	Nortrp	1.20	3.9	6	798	30⅞	30½	30⅞	+ ½
64	31¾	Norton	2.00	4.0	14	6722	54¼	48¾	49½	- 4½
78⅜	58	Nynex	4.04	6.3	10	1570	64	63	64	+ 1¼
— O — O — O —										
1¾	⅞	OakInd		...	10	814	1¼	1⅛	1⅛	...
38⅞	22¼	OcciPet	2.50	9.6	22	4599	26	25¾	26	+ ¼
23¼	16½	OhioEd	1.96	10.8	9	1853	18¼	17¾	18⅛	+ ⅜
22	11¼	OhMatr	.60	3.2	14	165	18¾	18½	18½	- ⅛
19	9⅛	Oxford	.50	5.0	...	11	10¼	10	10	⅛
— P — Q —										
33¾	24	PacTel	1.76	6.1	11	2519	28⅞	28	28⅞	+ ¼
36	13⅛	PainWb	.52	3.3	15	1792	15⅞	15⅝	15⅞	+ ¼
5½	2⅜	PanAm		...	...	1595	2⅝	2½	2⅝	+ ⅛
27½	9⅝	PayCsh	.16	.6	32	454	26¾	26⅝	26¾	...
66	35¼	Penney	2.00	4.4	10	2748	46¼	45⅝	45¾	+ ¼
42¼	25½	PepsiCo	.84	2.4	14	7606	35	34	35	+ 1
56	23½	PhelpD	.80	2.0	4	1346	40⅝	39½	40	- ⅝
124½	77⅛	PhilMr	3.60	4.0	10	4196	90⅛	88¾	89⅞	+ ⅞
26½	7½	PhlVH	.28	2.7	6	253	10⅜	9⅞	10⅜	+ ¼
14⅜	4¾	Pier 1	.08	.8	19	1379	10½	10	10½	+ ⅜
103½	60	ProctG	2.80	3.8	23	3679	73⅜	71⅞	73¼	+ 1½
9¾	3⅜	Pullmn	.12	1.3	24	36948	9⅛	8⅞	9	+ 1½
57⅛	31¾	QuakrO	1.00	2.2	16	2018	46	44¾	45⅞	+ 1⅛
14¼	4¼	Quanex		...	11	681	12⅝	12	12⅝	- ¼
— R — R — R —										
94	57⅜	RalsPur	1.50	2.0	13	1132	76⅞	75⅞	76⅜	+ ¾
84⅞	57¼	Raythn	2.00	3.0	10	480	66⅜	65⅝	66¼	+ ½
12	5¼	Redmn	.36	4.6	...	339	8¼	7⅞	7⅞	- ⅜
11½	4½	RelGrp	.24	4.0	4	25	6	5⅞	6	...
55¼	36¼	RepNY	1.20	2.7	10	184	44½	44⅜	44½	...
18¼	14¼	RochG	1.50	8.5	11	131	17⅝	17½	17⅝	+ ⅛
29⅞	14¼	Rockwl	.72	3.4	7	1965	21¼	20	20⅞	+ 1
39⅛	19¾	Rorer s	.80	2.1	21	3982	37⅜	36⅜	37¼	+ 1⅛
— S — S — S —										
38¾	16⅝	Salomn	.64	2.7	22	6050	23¾	22¾	23⅝	+ ½
30½	12	SeaCnt	.30e	1.2	4	383	25⅛	24½	25⅛	+ ½
59½	29¾	Sears	2.00	5.6	9	5269	36	35¼	36	+ ⅞
60	39	Smuckr	.88	1.6	17	10	54¾	54⅛	54⅛	- ⅞
13¼	6½	StdPac	1.20e	11.6	6	514	10⅜	10⅛	10⅜	+ ¼
48¾	23	Syntex	1.30	3.3	16	2362	39⅛	38⅛	39	+ ½
— T — T — T —										
78½	53	TDK	.54e	.7	...	236	81 u	79¼	80½	+ 9
70	37	TRW	1.60	3.5	10	685	45¾	45⅛	45½	+ ¼
56½	28	Tandy	.60	1.4	13	3375	42⅞	42	42¾	- ⅛
3⅞	1⅝	Telcom		...	18	4	1¾	1⅝	1¾	...
62½	36⅛	Tennco	3.04	6.4	...	3533	47¼	46⅝	47¼	+ ⅝
52½	26⅞	Texaco	3.00	6.3	13	7688	47½	46¼	47½	+ ⅞
80¼	36¼	TexInst	.72	1.7	14	7184	42¾	41⅞	42¼	+ ⅝
34⅜	24⅝	TexUtil	2.88	10.3	6	5765	28	27⅝	28	+ ¼
10½	4	Tidwtr		...	...	244	6¾	6⅝	6¾	+ ⅛
41	14½	Tiffany	.05e	.1	17	172	33⅞	33⅜	33⅜	- ¼
116⅞	65¾	Time	1.00	1.0	21	1304	98¾	96⅝	98½	+ 1¾
36¾	21¾	Trchmk	1.20	3.9	10	343	31¼	31	31⅛	+ ⅛
42¾	22	ToyRU		...	23	2153	37⅜	36¼	37⅛	+ ⅜
36¼	14	TWA		...	...	273	34¼	33⅝	34¼	+ ½
13½	4⅞	TranEx	.88	13.3	...	250	6⅝	6½	6⅝	+ ⅛
48⅞	30¾	Travler	2.40	7.1	10	7726	34⅛	33¼	33⅞	- 1¼
49¾	29½	Tribune	.76	2.1	16	1168	36¾	36⅛	36⅝	+ ⅛
44¼	20¼	Trinova	.56	2.1	11	2049	26¾	26⅛	26¼	- ½
15⅛	7	Tultex	.36	4.1	10	206	8⅞	8¾	8¾	- ⅛
— U — U — U —										
105⅞	55	UAL Cp		...	13	5397	94½	93¼	93¾	+ ½
27⅜	15⅜	UNUM	.48	2.1	11	284	23⅝	23¼	23¼	...
39⅜	21	USX	1.20	3.9	18	2896	30¾	30¼	30⅝	...
37⅜	10⅜	Ultmte		...	8	198	10⅞	10⅝	10⅞	+ ⅛
47⅝	26	UnCmp	1.24	3.7	9	1427	34⅛	33⅞	33⅞	- ⅛
9½	4	UnionC		...	21	52	9¼	9	9⅛	+ ⅛
86⅝	45⅜	UnPac	2.00	3.4	11	2457	59⅜	58½	58¾	- ⅜
18¼	9¼	UBrnd s	.20	1.2	12	83	16⅜	16	16¼	...
18¾	10¼	UnitInd	.64	4.4	12	45	14¾	14½	14⅝	...
53½	26	UsairG	.12	.3	9	2011	36½	35¾	36⅛	...
60½	30	UnTech	1.60	4.3	7	3005	37	36⅜	37	+ ¼
34⅜	23½	UniTel	1.92	6.0	26	1590	32¼	321¾	32¼	+ ⅜
— V — V — V —										
48¼	22	Vf Cp	.84	2.9	10	423	28¾	28⅜	28½	+ ⅛
3⅞	2	Varity		...	12	2516	3¼	3⅛	3¼	+ ⅛
42⅞	20	WalMrt	.16	.5	27	4611	32	31¼	31⅞	+ ¼
44⅞	24¾	Walgrn	.60	1.9	16	905	32¼	31⅞	32⅛	+ ¼
85	50	Xerox	3.00	5.7	10	2368	52⅞	52¼	52¾	+ ⅝
33⅝	10	ZenithE		...	...	1009	23⅛	22½	22⅞	...
11¼	7⅝	Zweig	1.05e	10.0	...	509	10⅝	10⅜	10½	...

STOCK MARKET DATA — July 28, 199Z

Major Indexes

HIGH	LOW (12 MOS)		CLOSE	NET CH	% CH	12 MO CH	%	FROM 12/31	%
DOW JONES AVERAGES									
2722.42	1738.74	**30 Industrials**	2082.33	+ 28.63	+ 1.39	- 485.11	- 18.89	+ 143.50	+ 7.40
1101.16	661.00	**20 Transportation**	863.05	+ 7.32	+ 0.86	- 213.21	- 19.81	+ 114.19	+ 15.25
213.79	160.98	**15 Utilities**	178.88	+ 2.20	+ 1.25	- 22.82	- 11.31	+ 3.80	+ 2.17
992.21	653.76	**65 Composite**	776.11	+ 9.34	+ 1.22	- 174.08	- 18.32	+ 61.84	+ 8.66
NEW YORK STOCK EXCHANGE									
187.99	125.91	**Composite**	150.40	+ 1.66	+ 1.12	- 27.92	- 15.66	+ 12.17	+ 8.80
231.05	149.43	**Industrials**	181.93	+ 2.18	+ 1.21	- 37.94	- 17.26	+ 14.89	+ 8.91
80.22	61.63	**Utilities**	70.83	+ 0.57	+ 0.81	- 3.86	- 5.17	+ 3.52	+ 5.23
168.20	104.76	**Transportation**	133.86	+ 1.32	+ 1.00	- 28.72	- 17.67	+ 15.29	+ 12.90
165.36	107.39	**Finance**	128.72	+ 1.13	+ 0.89	- 25.60	- 16.59	+ 14.59	+ 12.35

III. Use the correct form of the key word in parentheses.

1. (expensive, cheap) We have three kinds. This one is the most _____; this one is medium-priced, and this one is the _____.

2. (price) He bought the highest- _____ model.

3. (security) I think the best _____ you can buy is this one.

4. (share) She owns a hundred _____ of Autosystem stock.

5. (safe) I think a savings account is the _____ kind of investment.

6. (broker) A _____ is a kind of agent who works for a brokerage firm.

7. (gain) My USTEL stock _____ three points yesterday.

8. (trend) I think you'll see a new _____ in the market.

9. (issue) Do you think they will ever re- _____ the Susan B. Anthony one-dollar coin?

10. (dividend) _____ can be expressed in dollars or in percentage.

11. (yield) The current _____ on our N.O.W account is 7.5%.

IV. Use the correct form of one of the key words in these sentences.

1. A large box that can be locked and is used for storing valuable things is a _____.

2. My _____ is D.P. Dutton.

3. Did your stock _____ or lose today?

4. Although she was wearing very _____ clothing, her perfume was _____.

5. What a _____ to pay!

6. The _____ in car-buying is toward the domestic models, and away from imports.

7. The Post Office has _____ a new airmail stamp.

8. Your _____ check is in the mail.

9. The principal _____ holder owns 42% of the shares.

10. SEC stands for _____ and Exchange Commission, a U.S. government agency.

11. Another word for _____ is "give".

46

Budgeting and Accounting

Everyone would agree that it is easy to spend money — sometimes too easy — and it is difficult to save money. And who has not said, after **counting** the money in his purse, "Where did my money go?" So before and after earning, spending and saving, people and businesses turn to paper and pencil — and now to computers — to plan what is going to happen with their money and **account** for what is happening or has happened to it.

A financial plan is called a budget, and our language has many phrases related to our budgets — staying within the budget, living within one's means, over-spending, cost over-runs, and budget deficits, for example.

This universal problem affects not only the individual, but all **entities** — small businesses, big corporations, nonprofit organizations, and of course, the government. Many politicians have

47

Federal Budget

INCOME

INCOME TAX

OTHER

BORROWING

EXCISE TAX

CORPORATE TAX

SOCIAL SECURITY

EXPENSES

INDIVIDUAL BENEFITS

GOVERNMENT OPERATIONS

INTEREST ON DEBT

STATE AND LOCAL GRANTS

MILITARY

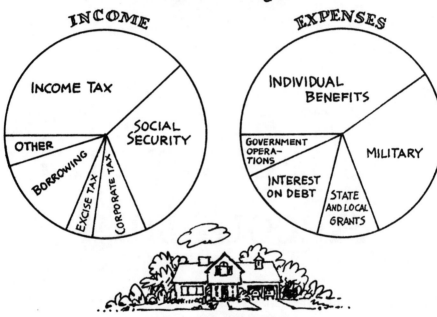

Family Budget

INCOME

JOE'S SALARY

INCOME INTEREST

DIVIDENDS

MARY'S SALARY

EXPENSES

SAVINGS

CAR PAYMENTS

MORTGAGE

COLLEGE LOAN

RECREATION

FOOD

UTILITIES

TAXES

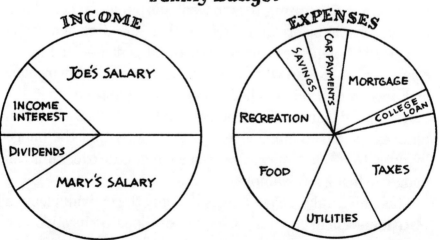

48

made many speeches about cost over-runs and budget **deficits** caused by expenses being greater than income. Husbands and wives worry about living within their means, and parents caution children about over-spending their **allowances**.

A budget is, quite simply, a **forecast** of what the **revenue** will be (how much money will come in) and what the **expenses** will be (how much money will go out). Some expenses are the result of purchases, and accountants call these purchases expenditures. If the budget is for a profit-making entity, the revenue should exceed the expenses and the **bottom line** should show a profit. The family hopes to have a balanced budget, and politicians often demand that the government balance its budget, too.

Budgets are prepared for certain periods of time. For example, a one-year accounting period is called a **fiscal** year. When the year begins it then becomes the task of the bookkeeper to record or enter the income and expense in journals and ledgers. The accountant then, in a sense, counts up and analyzes the financial status and the financial progress of the entity. The financial status is shown in a balance sheet which shows the **assets** (what is owned) and the **liabilities** (what is owed) and the **equities** (how much capital the business has). The accountant prepares a financial statement which has, in addition to the balance sheet, the income statement, which shows the important bottom line and the entity's profit or loss.

Key words

count	deficit	revenue	fiscal	liability
account	allowance	expense	asset	
entities	forecast	bottom line	equity	

I. Use one of the key words above in the following sentences. Use each word only once.

    1. If money is spent, it is an _____.

    2. Money that is earned is _____.

    3. If expenses are greater than revenues, there is a _____.

4. Money that is owed is a _____.
5. Money that is owned is an _____.
6. Assets minus liabilities equal _____, or capital.
7. A balanced budget shows a _____ that does not have a deficit.
8. Let's _____ our money and see how much we have.
9. Corporations are _____.
10. He gives his children an _____ of $10.00 each per week.
11. The government's _____ year begins July 1.
12. A look into the future can be called a _____.
13. "You've got to _____ for every centavo you've spent," said the angry woman.

II. Underline the correct form of the key word.

1. If there is a (deficits, deficit), it may be because the (revenues, revenue) are (deficient, deficiently).
2. The (fiscally, fiscal) year may not be the same as the calendar year.
3. We get a daily (allow, allowing, allowance) for food and lodging when we are traveling.
4. A person who makes a forecast is a (forecastist, forecaster).
5. I need to approve all (expensive, expenditures).
6. The (accounter, accountant, accountist) has set up a new system of (accountable, accounts).
7. (Asset, Assets) = liabilities – the owners' equity.
8. Yesterday I (count, countered, counted) all our cash.
9. An (entity, entities) is something that exists; therefore a non-(entity, entities) doesn't exist.

50

MONEY, INC

Balance Sheet as of December 31, 199Z

Assets

Current assets

Cash	$ 31,650	
Securities	2,750	
Accounts receivable	58,365	
Inventory	135,120	
Total current assets		$227,885

Noncurrent assets

Property and plant	270,500	
less depreciation	120,800	
Total noncurrent assets		149,700

Investments		10,000
Total assets		**$387,585**

Equities

Current liabilities

Accounts payable	$ 65,750	
Estimated Tax	13,475	
Others	8,900	
Total current liabilities		$ 88,125

Noncurrent liabilities

Mortgage bonds payable	25,000	
Total liabilities		113,125

Shareholders' equity

Common Stock	$150,000	
Retained earnings	124,460	
Total shareholders' equity		274,460
Total equities		**$387,585**

III. Use the correct form of the key word in parentheses.

1. (deficit) The United States has a trade _____ with Japan.
2. (liability) Our assets are greater than our _____.
3. (allow) We are not _____ to spend any money in that account.
4. (account) There's something wrong here, and I can't _____ for it.
5. (count) The king is in the counting house, _____ all his money.
6. (revenue) For the government, taxes are _____.
7. (fiscal) To be in good financial health is to be _____ healthy.
8. (Forecast) _____ the weather will never be an exact science.
9. (expenditure) The military accounts for 40% of the government's _____.

IV. Use a key word in these sentences.

1. The _____ for tomorrow is for more rain.
2. The _____ for meals is $20 a day.
3. The _____ is this: We lost money last year.
4. To be "in the black" is to show a profit. To be "in the red" is to have a _____.
5. The government agency responsible for collecting taxes is the Internal _____ Service.
6. This administration is _____ irresponsible. Vote for me and for _____ responsibility.
7. Cash, equipment, and buildings are _____.
8. After we have paid all our _____, the balance is the owners' _____.
9. Don't _____ your chickens before they hatch.
10. "You're nothing!" he shouted, "You're a non- _____!"
11. We've got to reduce our _____ this month, or we'll be in the red again.
12. "What _____ should I charge this expenditure to?" asked the bookkeeper.

52

Insurance

The purpose of insurance is to provide financial **compensation** to people and organizations when something unexpected or **disastrous** happens and the result is financial loss. In a way, insurance companies offer **protection** so that an accident, a severe health problem, a fire, or a natural disaster such as a flood, will not result in a financial disaster to a family or business entity.

The first form of insurance **coverage** was marine insurance, provided by Lloyd's of London in 1689 to protect shipowners and merchants from loss if a ship sank with its cargo. Nowadays many different kinds of **policies** are offered.

Policyholders commonly insure their health, their property (especially homes and autos), and their lives, and they also carry liability protection. Liability insurance protects the policyholder against a legal suit in which somebody may **sue** the policyholder, claiming that the policyholder was responsible for damage that the plaintiff (the person who sues) suffered.

For families, it is important of course, to protect their major investments, and so they insure their homes against fire and the family car against damage from accidents. In recent years, automobile insurance has become very expensive, especially liability protection, and in many places it is **compulsory**, which means the family members cannot use the car if they do not have insurance. For some families in the United States, especially those with teen-age drivers, the **premiums** may be well over $1,000 a year. The insurance can cost more than the car!

Health insurance is also very important to the family because the cost of health care has become very high. One way in which the cost of the premiums can be reduced is to carry a high **deductible** amount. This means that the family would pay for the first $500, for example, of the costs, and the insurance company would then pay for the rest, after the first $500 has been deducted. A form of health insurance called **disability** insurance is also carried by many working people. If they are disabled and cannot work — perhaps because of a broken arm — they will receive money from the insurance company.

Life insurance is paid when a person dies. The **beneficiaries** of the policy will receive money to cover the lost wages that the dead person can no longer earn. This kind of protection is especially important for families with small children where it may be difficult for the surviving parent to work and care for the children.

Another kind of insurance provides the financial security a person needs when he or she retires and no longer earns wages or a salary. Most people, while they are working, belong to a retirement plan, and then when they retire, they receive a **pension**. For many older people the arrival of their monthly pension check is a very important event. In many countries there is a compulsory government plan often called national insurance or social security.

Key words

compensation	coverage	compulsory	disability
disaster	policy	premium	beneficiary
protection	sue	deductible	pension

I. Use one of the key words above in the following sentences. Use each key word only once.

    1. She's retired now and living on her _____.

    2. In this state you must have liability insurance; it's _____.

3. A good insurance _____ will give your family _____ against financial disaster.
4. What a _____! Everything was destroyed.
5. He can't work now, but he has _____ insurance so he is receiving some money.
6. His wife was the _____ of his life insurance policy.
7. The _____ for this policy is only $15 a month, and for that you get _____ of $10,000.
8. He threatened to take them to court and _____ them for a million dollars.
9. This policy carries a $200 _____ amount. After you pay $200, the company will pay the rest.
10. This check is little _____ for the loss of your husband, Mrs. Johnson, but I'm sure he would be happy to know that you won't have any financial worries.

II. Underline the correct form of the key word.

1. A person who receives a pension can be called a (pensioner, pension).
2. A person who receives benefits is a (beneficient, beneficiary).
3. A person who receives disability payments is (disabling, disabled).
4. A deductible amount is a (deducter, deduction).
5. The person who owns the policy is the (policeman, policyholder, politician).
6. A person who has insurance coverage is (covering, covered).
7. A person who has protection is (protector, protected).
8. A person who receives compensation is (compensating, compensated).
9. A person who (sue, sues, sueing) files a legal suit.
10. The results of a disaster are (disasterous, disastrous).
11. In this country, participation in national insurance is (compulsive, compulsory).
12. Installment payments are sometimes called (premium, premiums).

III. Use the correct form of the key word in parentheses.

1. (policy) He owns several _____.

2. (beneficiary) She listed her children as _____.

3. (cover) This policy will give you complete _____.

4. (compensate) You will be _____ for your work.

5. (protect) Your family will be fully _____ if you should die.

6. (disable) He is a _____ veteran of the Viet Nam War.

7. (deduct) After _____ your expenses from your allowance, you should write the balance due here.

8. (disaster) The stock market crash of 1987 was _____.

9. (sue) This liability coverage will protect you in case you are

_____.

10. (compulsory) I don't have to do that; it's not _____.

IV. Use one of the key words in these sentences.

1. My automobile insurance _____ cost me about $500 last year.

2. The sinking of the Titanic, with the loss of hundreds of lives, was one of the worst _____ of the twentieth century.

3. "Don't worry, I'll _____ you," said the little boy to his sister.

4. As the _____ of her life insurance policy, he received $50,000 when she died.

5. The _____ should be paid by the end of the month.

6. "I'll _____ you for that!" shouted the angry man.

7. All the employees have to pay into the company's _____ fund. Each month the company _____ 10% from its employee's paychecks. It is a _____ deduction. The employees can retire at age 65.

8. He has been _____ and unable to work for the last five years.

9. I expected to be _____ for my services. I didn't think I was working for nothing.

10. All the TV networks will cover the election tonight. The _____ will begin at 6 p.m. and go all night long.

57

GAMBLING

One of the most common verbs in the English language is **"bet."** English speakers frequently use it simply to mean "think" or "believe," and in some areas of the United States "you bet" means "okay" or "yes." But for the gambler, the word "bet" is almost always followed by phrases such as "two dollars." The gambler's bet is a **wager**, and his goal is to **win** the wager and make money, just as a laborer earns wages or a businessman makes a profit. However, gambling is a risky way to earn a living, and in many places gambling is not permitted; it is **illegal**.

There are many ways to gamble, and almost everyone has gambled in one way or another. Probably the most common form of gambling is the lottery, in which large numbers of people buy tickets with a number on them, hoping to get the **lucky** number and win a **huge** sum of money, becoming instant millionaires. Winning at the lottery is purely a matter of luck.

People also like to bet on sporting events, where, in addition to luck, a little knowledge may be helpful. For most people this is done with friends who make a wager on the outcome of a football game, for example. One sport in particular, horse racing, has become more of a gambling event than a sporting event.

Much of the vocabulary of gambling has developed from horse racing. In horse racing, there is a system based on the past performance of the horses. A horse that has done well in the past and is expected to win the race is the **favorite**. People who accept bets (bookmakers or bookies) give **odds** on the horse's chance of winning. It is not so risky to bet on the favorite, and so a person who places a bet on the favorite would not win as much money as the person who makes a bet on a horse that has not done so well in the past. Betting on a horse with a poor or unknown record is sometimes called "taking a long shot," and the horse itself is sometimes called a "dark horse."

Many games have also become associated with gambling. One that is especially well known is the card game called poker. As in horse racing, a lot of words used in poker have become popular idioms. Two of the most common ones are **"pass,"** when a player does not want to bet, and **"fold,"** when a player does not want to continue the game, perhaps because the **stakes** are too high, meaning that the results for winners and losers will be large winnings and large losses.

There are many other games of **chance**, from simple games like Bingo to the more complicated ones that use dice or machines such as roulette wheels and slot machines — also known as "one-armed bandits."

Regardless of the kind of gambling, it is Lady Luck who, more often than not, gives and takes pennies and **fortunes**.

ROCKSBORO ENTRIES

First Post 1:00 (SST)

FIRST—32,000, cl, 4YO up, 1 mi.

Nimrod	122	Sally's Girl	122
Passing Ships	112	Top Gun	116
Natty's Nag	114	Pumpkin	107

SECOND—20,000, cl, 3YO up, 1 mi.

Candy Stripe	110	Pink Lady	117
Native Jogger	115	True Fox	119
Mrs. Robinson	115	Yellow Rose	107

THIRD—47,000, 3YO up, 11-16 mi.
Heart Throb Handicap

Mr. Snow	122	Mere de Ver	116
Walkabout	108	Tequila	108
Tried 'n' True	116	Dark Prince	122
Wenlock	114	Tammy True	111
Byron's Choice	122	Al sheik	117

DOG WORLD ENTRIES

For Friday
POST TIME — 7:30 P.M.
BEST — LASER LIPS, 2nd
FIRST — 5-16 MILE (M)

Uncle Joe	6-1	Sir Speed	8-1
Dawn Dream	4-1	Papillon	12-1
Ebony Gal	10-1	AB's Bash	8-1
Guy B	3-1	Twinkie Toes	5-1

SECOND—Y.C. (D)

Kool Kidde	15-1	Ripe Tide	10-1
Freddie	4-1	Laser Lips	5-2
Tern Styles	9-2	Classy Coke	6-1
Watts Line	6-1	Marko Polo	3-1

$$ LOTTERIES $$

Thursday's 5-State Lottery: 2430
PAYOFFS BASED ON $1 BETS

Exact Order		Any Order	
All 4 digits	$3,846	All 4 digits	$160
First or last 3	$538	First 3 digits	$90
Any 2 digits	$46	Last 3 digits	$90
Any 1 digit	$5		

WED. MEGABUCKS:	5	10	12	24	32	34
MEGABUCKS JACKPOT:						$7,828,900

(two winners)

ROCKSBORO RESULTS

Weather Clear, Track Fast

FIRST—18,000, cl, 4YO up, 7f

Tarzan B	9.00	6.20	3.00
Hot Lips		13.40	4.80
Starwalker			2.60

Winning Jockeys — Gomez, Browne, Sanchez. Off 1:00
Time 1:24 1-5.

EXACTA—$105.00

SECOND—29,000, alc, 3YO up, 11-16 mi. tf.

Guilford Girl	22.20	7.00	4.40
Crass Tail		7.60	4.20
Foggy Days			2.60

Winning Jockeys—Snodgrass, El Gata, Karlsson. Off 1:26
Time 1:43 2-5.

DOUBLE—$122.20 EX—145.80

THIRD—31,000, alc, 3YO up, 11-16 mi.

Dumb Dutch	4.40	2.60	2.10
Phancy Pants		3.20	2.10
Whiz Bang			2.10

Winning Jockeys—Pope, Cervantes, Goethe. Off 1:32,
Time 1:43 Scratched—Tyler's Hope, Merry Blue, Laser Lass

DOUBLE—$7.20 PIC-6—$4090.00
PIC-6 (5) $27.00

DOG WORLD RESULTS

EVENING PROGRAM
FIRST—5-16(B)T—31.69

3 Sugar Plumb	5.00	3.40	3.60
8 Pacemaker		9.00	10.20
5 Satisfaction			3.80

QUIN—$24.20 TRI-102.20

SECOND—YC(B)T—40.27

7 Wonder Bar	8.60	2.80	2.80
8 Pudgey		2.60	2.80
4 Enchanter			5.20

QUIN—$27.60 TRI—440.80
TWIN TRI C'OVER $18,844.00

Key words

bet	legalizing	favorite	folded
wagered	unlucky	won	huge
pass	stakes	odds	chance
fortune			

I. Use the key words above in the following sentences. Use each word only once.

1. I'll _____ you $10 that the Boston Celtics will beat the Los Angeles Lakers in tonight's game.

2. He made a _____ fortune by investing in computers.

3. You are gambling with your life when you drink and drive, and those _____ are too high for anyone to pay.

4. If you are betting on Number 5, the _____ are 3 to 1.

5. Games of _____ bore me because there is no skill involved.

6. How many games has the school basketball team _____ so far?

7. When I bet on a horse, I usually select the _____, although occasionally I will put my money on a dark horse just for fun.

8. Thanks for the invitation tonight, but I'll have to _____ as I have a lot of work to complete before tomorrow's meeting.

9. The Kennedy family _____ came from investments in the railroads.

10. Franklin often went to the race track but he never _____ more than ten dollars.

11. I wasn't surprised that his company _____; it had been overextended in its loans for months.

12. A few states are now _____ gambling to provide added sources of state revenues.

13. This is the thirteenth sentence. Many people think thirteen is an _____ number.

II. Underline the correct form of the key word.

1. (Bet, Betting, Bettors) can become an addiction. Some people gamble away all their money.

61

2. The lottery (won, winner, winnings) gave all his prize money to UNICEF.
3. It is (illegal, illegalized, illegally) in any state for children to gamble.
4. Although it didn't look like rain when I left home this morning, (lucky, luck, luckily) I brought an umbrella.
5. That bear is the (hugest, huge, hugely) animal I have ever seen.
6. I don't understand why you (pass, passed, passing) in the last bridge hand because I thought you had a lot of points and wanted to raise the bid.
7. Companies that cannot keep up with the competition are forced to (fold, folding) or to sell out to larger corporations.
8. The (favorite, favoritism) came in third.
9. The (oddity, oddly, odds) are not in his favor.
10. I didn't plan on meeting her; I met her by (chance, chanced).
11. It was (fortune, fortunate, fortunately) that we were able to meet.
12. I am (staked, staking, stakes) my reputation on your winning the race.
13. He is crazy to (wager, wagered, wagering) such a large sum on such a long shot.

III. Use the correct form of the key word in parentheses.

1. 1. (bet) He _____ and lost all his salary last night at the casino and I'll _____ he will do same thing again next payday.
2. (fold) So far, all of her businesses have _____.
3. (win) You must declare all your lottery _____ to the government.
4. (stake) Because his brother _____ him to $100, Albert was able to enter the game and win.
5. (fortune) That was a very un _____ move you made; I can now win the game.
6. (legal) The use of marijuana has been _____ only for medical and research purposes.
7. (wager) He was drunk when he made that _____.
8. (huge) The university is grateful for her _____ contribution.

62

9. (odds) I'll give _____ of three to one that he doesn't come on time.

10. (favorite) Teachers try not to have _____ students because favoritism is not fair.

11. (luck) Some people carry _____charms, such as a four leaf clover, a rabbit's foot, or a new penny, hoping these things will bring good _____.

12. (pass) In the card game of bridge, three _____ automatically require that a new hand be dealt.

13. (chance) What do you think the Democratic candidate's _____ are for winning the election this time?

IV. Use the key word in these sentences.

1. It is better to quit while you are ahead in this game; the _____ will only get higher and higher.

2. The _____ are very high that Prince Charles will replace Queen Elizabeth as Britain's monarch.

3. Would you like to take a _____ on the lottery? The tickets are only 300 pesos.

4. Since I don't know, I'll _____ on that question.

5. For me there is a _____ difference between fresh, brewed coffee and instant coffee.

6. Every Olympic athlete dreams of _____ a gold medal.

7. Many investors lost _____ in the autumn stock market fall known as Black Monday.

8. When a business _____, we say it has "gone out of business."

9. He bet on number three and won; his two-dollar _____ paid twenty dollars.

10. Four is usually my _____ number but tonight I am losing.

11. It is usually safe to bet on the _____, as that horse nearly always wins something.

12. He is in the country _____ and is afraid of being deported if found without a passport.

13. To place a wager, gamblers call a bookmaker to _____ on the team, number, horse or whatever they hope will win money for them.

63

Changing Money

Changing money can mean two things: changing a large bill or coin into smaller bills or coins, such as changing a five-dollar bill into five ones, or exchanging two currencies, for example, dollars for pounds. In the first instance, there are times when a person needs small **change** (we usually think of small change as coins) or when a person has a high-**denomination** banknote and wants to get smaller denominations. In the second instance, changing currencies, we enter into the very complex world of the foreign exchange market.

Just as our world does not have only one language as the medium of communication, neither do we have a single **monetary** system as the medium of international exchange. Any traveler experiences this when he goes to another country. One of the first things he must do is find a place to **convert** his money, and one of his first questions will be, "What is the exchange rate?" As we all know, exchange rates can vary from day to day and from place to place. One place in particular, the black market, often has a rate that is better than the **official** rate.

As our world shrinks and it becomes easier to carry out trade across international boundaries, the **volume** of trade increases, and therefore the **flow** of money increases. Large numbers of businesses become involved in **exporting** and **importing** goods. If a businessman exports his product to another country he is going to receive money from a company or person in another country. Businessmen, therefore, need the services of a money changer, and so they turn to banks. A bank, then, becomes the middleman, arranging for the exchange of money across national boundaries.

In the world of international trade, some currencies are more desireable than others. The currencies of some countries are not very **stable**, and **inflation** may cause the currency to continuously lose its value. In some cases a government may officially devalue its own currency. In other cases the currency may be allowed to **float**, meaning that the value of the currency will go up or down according to the demand for it.

Currencies are traded on the foreign exchange market, which is an international market with major centers in London, Frankfurt, Zurich, Tokyo, Hong Kong, and New York. At these markets traders buy and sell currencies from each other. Many of the traders are from international banks and large corporations, but there are also individual **speculators** who are trying to make a profit by watching the exchange rates very closely and buying and selling currencies — hoping to buy low and sell high.

NAMES OF THE WORLD'S CURRENCIES

Afghani	◆	Afghanistan
Baht	◆	Thailand
Balboa	◆	Panama
Birr	◆	Ethiopia
Bolivar	◆	Venezuela
Cedi	◆	Ghana
Colon	◆	El Salvador, Costa Rica
Cordoba	◆	Nicaragua
Cruzeiro	◆	Brazil
Dalasi	◆	Gambia
Dinar	◆	Algeria, Iraq, Kuwait, Libya, Tunisia, South Yemen, Jordan, Bahrain, Yugoslavia
Dirham	◆	United Arab Emirates, Morocco
Dobra	◆	Sao Tome

Dollar	◆	Australia, Canada, USA, New Zealand, Liberia, Zimbabwe, Bahamas, Bermuda, Barbados, Guyana, Belize, Brunei, Jamaica, Fiji, Singapore, Taiwan, Trinidad and Tobago
Drachma	◆	Greece
Escudo	◆	Portugal, Cape Verde
Forint	◆	Hungary
Franc	◆	France, Switzerland, Belgium, Luxembourg, Benin, Burundi, Cameroon, Central African Republic, Chad, Comoro Islands, Congo, Djibouti, Gabon, Ivory Coast, Madagascar, Mali, Niger, Rwanda, Senegal, Togo
Gourde	◆	Haiti
Guarani	◆	Paraguay
Guilder	◆	Netherlands, Surinam
Kina	◆	Papua New Guinea
Kip	◆	Laos
Koruna	◆	Czechoslovakia
Krona	◆	Sweden, Iceland
Krone	◆	Denmark, Norway
Kwacha	◆	Malawi, Zambia
Kwanza	◆	Angola
Kyat	◆	Burma
Lek	◆	Albania
Lempira	◆	Honduras
Leone	◆	Sierra Leone
Leu	◆	Romania
Lev	◆	Bulgaria
Lilangeni	◆	Swaziland
Lira	◆	Italy, Turkey
Loti	◆	Lesotho
Mark	◆	West Germany, East Germany
Markaa	◆	Finland

Metical	◆	Mozambique
Naira	◆	Nigeria
Ouguiya	◆	Mauritania
Peseta	◆	Spain
Peso	◆	Argentian, Bolivia, Chile, Colombia, Cuba, Dominican Republic, Mexico, Uruguay, Philippines, Guinea-Bissau
Pound	◆	United Kingdom, Ireland, Egypt, Syria, Malta, Cyprus, Lebanon, Sudan
Pula	◆	Botswana
Quetzal	◆	Guatemala
Rand	◆	South Africa
Rial	◆	Iran, Oman, North Yemen
Riel	◆	Kampuchea
Ringgit	◆	Malaysia
Riyal	◆	Saudi Arabia, Qatar
Ruble	◆	USSR
Rupee	◆	India, Pakistan, Nepal, Sir Lanka, Mauritius, Seychelles
Rupiah	◆	Indonesia
Schilling	◆	Austria
Shekel	◆	Israel
Shilling	◆	Kenya, Somalia, Tanzania, Uganda
Sol	◆	Peru
Sucre	◆	Ecuador
Syli	◆	Guinea
Taka	◆	Bangladesh
Tala	◆	Western Samoa
Tugrik	◆	Mongolia
Won	◆	South Korea, North Korea
Yen	◆	Japan
Yuan	◆	China
Zaire	◆	Zaire
Zloti	◆	Poland

Key words

change	convert	flow	stable
denomination	official	exports	inflation
monetary	volume	imports	float
			speculate

I. Use one of the key words above in the following sentences. Use each word only once.

1. Goods that go out of the country are _____, and goods that come in are _____.

2. The _____ exchange rate is 3.5 to 1, but on the black market you can get 3.8.

3. The IMF is the International _____Fund. It loans money for development.

4. Excuse me, sir. Can you _____ a 10,000-yen note?

5. The government is concerned about the _____ of capital out of the country.

6. The _____ of imports has increased again this year.

7. I'd like to _____ pounds to francs.

8. What is the highest _____ of the West German Mark?

9. _____ is reducing the purchasing power of our earnings.

10. The government has decided to _____ the lira rather than devalue it.

11. The stock market seems to be _____ again after a series of ups and downs.

12. He thought the peso would go up, so he decided to _____ and buy several million.

II. Use the correct form of the key word in parentheses.

1. I need some coins. Do you have any (changes, change)?

2. Last year the U.S. (exported, export) less than it (imported, import).

3. With this conversion table, you can easily (convert, convertible) dollars and other currencies.

4. There has been a constant (float, flow, flowed) of dollars to other countries.

5. The new policy has not been (official, officially) announced.

6. Financial (stable, stability) is not easy to achieve.

7. I think the new policy is (inflation, inflationary).

8. (Speculator, Speculation) means taking a risk, hoping to make a large profit.

9. When a currency is (floating, flotation), its value rises and falls with supply and demand.

10. The Central Bank establishes (monetarily, monetary) policies.

III. Use the correct form of a key word in these sentences.

1. (import, export) He imports goods. He's an _____.
She exports goods. She's an _____.

2. (convert) Last week I _____ all my traveler's checks to rubles.

3. (change) I need some coins. Do you have any _____?

4. (denomination) He had bills of every _____ in his wallet.

5. (official) This will only be _____ when it is _____ approved by a government _____.

6. (stable) The president said that we had achieved economic _____.

7. (monetary) Several years ago the British modified their _____ system so that there are now 100 pence to the pound rather than 240.

8. (Inflation) _____ increases when demand exceeds supply.

9. (float) Just as currency can be _____, an exchange rate can be called a _____ exchange rate.

10. (Speculate) _____ are buying South African rands.

11. (flow, volume) There has been a constant _____ of dollars out of the country, and the _____ of imports has not decreased at all.

70

IV. Use a key word in each of these sentences.

1. I don't have any ＿＿＿＿＿＿＿＿. Can you lend me a few coins?

2. First he ＿＿＿＿＿＿＿＿ marks to pounds, and then he sold his pounds for yen. His ＿＿＿＿＿＿＿＿ brought him a profit of over twenty thousand dollars. Not bad, for a day's work.

3. Toyotas are ＿＿＿＿＿＿＿＿ by the Japanese to the U.S., and the U.S. ＿＿＿＿＿＿＿＿ Saabs from Sweden.

4. When Lee first arrived in Turkey the ＿＿＿＿＿＿＿＿ exchange rate was 14 lira to the dollar. Now it's over 1,000.

5. The prices of new cars have gone up by 30%, while the overall ＿＿＿＿＿＿＿＿ rate is only 10%.

6. The hero did not expect a ＿＿＿＿＿＿＿＿ reward. Nevertheless, he was pleased to receive the $5,000.

7. She asked for $1,000 in small ＿＿＿＿＿＿＿＿ — tens and twenties only.

8. The patient's condition has been ＿＿＿＿＿＿＿＿ for two days now, so we expect she will recover.

9. The empty boat was found ＿＿＿＿＿＿＿＿ on the water.

10. To increase or decrease the amount of sound on the radio, turn the ＿＿＿＿＿＿＿＿ knob.

11. The amount of water ＿＿＿＿＿＿＿＿ through the dam has decreased in the past few days.

Death and Taxes

It is sometimes said that the only sure things in life are death and taxes. Death is, of course, a certainty. Taxation exists wherever there is a government, and since virtually everyone lives under the goverment one of the world's 170 nations, taxes too are a certainty.

There are many kinds of taxes, but the two that are found almost everywhere are sales taxes and income taxes. A sales tax is paid when we buy something. It is usually **calculated** as a **percentage** (e.g., 5 per cent) of the price of the thing purchased. Income tax, which is also called **withholding** tax, is a tax people pay on their earnings.

Although there are many ways in which income taxes are collected, the system that is used in the United States is typical. A wage-earner's tax is based on a percentage of his earnings, and that percentage increases as the earnings increase. Employees are allowed a certain number of **exemptions**, which reduce their taxable income. Exemptions are given for the number of dependents (children and other non-working family members) that the worker supports. Tax tables are often used to calculate the amount that the employer should withhold from the employee's paycheck. Self-employed people or people with irregular incomes must **estimate** the amount of tax they will owe and pay it in installments.

April 15 is a well-known date in the United States. It is the deadline for **filing** tax returns with the Internal Revenue Service. Every person must report his **gross** income which is the total amount he earned, claim his deductions for exemptions and other deductible expenses, and then pay tax on his **net** taxable income. In simple terms, net equals gross minus deductions. In some cases, people choose to **itemize** their deductions if they have a lot of deductible expenses. They list, item by item, all the deductible expenses they have had during the year. Medical expenses, for example, are deductible. Every one hopes that after all the **computations** they will find they have paid too much in taxes, and the government will give them a **refund**.

The other certainty, death, brings an end to concerns about taxes, but the person who has died usually leaves some wealth behind for others to be concerned about. What is left — money and property — is called the estate, and directions for who shall **inherit** the estate are contained in the **will**. Many a novel and murder mystery has been written about the death and will of a rich old man whose final words are: "And to my personal secretary, Miss Muggeridge, I leave my entire fortune."

Department of the Treasury · Internal Revenue Service

Form
1040EZ

Income Tax Return for
Single filers with no dependents (0)   **1987**

OMB No. 1545-0675

Name & address	Use the IRS mailing label. If you don't have one, please print.	Please print your numbers like this:

Print your name above (first, initial, last)

Present home **address** (number and street). (If you have a P.O. box, see instructions.)

City, town, or post office, state, and ZIP code

Please print your numbers like this:
0 1 2 3 4 5 6 7 8 9

Your social security number

Please read the instructions for this form on the reverse side.

Yes No

Presidential Election Campaign Fund
Do you want $1 to go to this fund?

Note: *Checking "Yes" will not change your tax or reduce your refund.*

Dollars   Cents

Report your income

1 Total wages, salaries, and tips. This should be shown in Box 10 of your W-2 form(s). (Attach your W-2 form(s).)   1

2 Taxable interest income of $400 or less. If the total is more than $400, you cannot use Form 1040EZ.   2

Attach
Copy B of
Form(s)
W-2 here

3 Add line 1 and line 2. This is your **adjusted gross income**.   3

4 Can you be claimed as a dependent on another person's return?
  ☐ Yes. Do worksheet on back; enter amount from line E here.
  ☐ No. Enter 2,540 as your standard deduction.   4

5 Subtract line 4 from line 3.   5

6 If you checked the "Yes" box on line 4, enter 0.
  If you checked the "No" box on line 4, enter 1,900.
  This is your **personal exemption**.   6

7 Subtract line 6 from line 5. If line 6 is larger than line 5, enter 0 on line 7. This is your **taxable income**.   7

Figure your tax

8 Enter your Federal income tax withheld. This should be shown in Box 9 of your W-2 form(s).   8

9 Use the **single** column in the tax table on pages 32–37 of the Form 1040A instruction booklet to find the **tax** on the amount shown on **line 7** above. Enter the amount of tax.   9

Refund or amount you owe

Attach tax payment here

10 If line 8 is larger than line 9, subtract line 9 from line 8. Enter the **amount of your refund**.   10

11 If line 9 is larger than line 8, subtract line 8 from line 9. Enter the **amount you owe**. Attach check or money order for the full amount, payable to "Internal Revenue Service."   11

Sign your return

I have read this return. Under penalties of perjury, I declare that to the best of my knowledge and belief, the return is true, correct, and complete.

Your signature   Date

For IRS Use Only—Please do not write in boxes below.

Form **1040EZ** (1987)

Use this form if:	• Your filing status is single. • You are not 65 or over, OR blind.

Use this form if:
- Your filing status is single.
- You do not claim any dependents.
- You are not 65 or over, OR blind.
- Your taxable income is less than $50,000.
- You had **only** wages, salaries, and tips, and your taxable interest income was $400 or less. **Caution:** If you received tips (including allocated tips) that are not included in Box 14 of your W-2 form, you may not be able to use Form 1040EZ. See page 17 in the **Instructions for preparing 1040EZ and 1040A**. If you can't use this form, you must use Form 1040A or Form 1040. See pages 6 through 8 in the instruction booklet. If you are uncertain about your filing status, see page 9 of the booklet.

Completing your return

It will make it easier for us to process your return if you print your numbers (do not type) and keep them inside the boxes. Do not use dollar signs. You may find calculations easier if you round off cents to whole dollars. See page 15 of the instruction booklet for details.

Name & address

Use the mailing label we sent you. After you complete your return, carefully place the label in the name and address area. Mark through any errors on the label and print the correct information on the label. Use of the label saves processing time. If you don't have a label, print the information on the name and address lines. If your post office does not deliver mail to your street address and you have a P.O. box, enter your P.O. box number on the line for your present home address instead of your street address.

Presidential campaign fund

Congress set up this fund to help pay for Presidential election campaigns. You may have one of your tax dollars go to this fund by checking the "Yes" box. Checking the "Yes" box does not change the tax or refund shown on your return.

Report your income

Line 1. Enter on line 1 the total amount you received in wages, salaries, and tips. This should be shown in Box 10 of your 1987 wage statement(s), **Form W-2**. If you don't receive your W-2 form by February 15, contact your local IRS office. You must still report your earnings even if you don't get a Form W-2 from your employer. Attach the first copy or Copy B of your W-2 form(s) to your return.

Line 2. Enter on line 2 the total taxable interest income you received from all sources, such as banks, savings and loans, and credit unions. You should receive a **Form 1099-INT** from each institution that paid you interest. You cannot use Form 1040EZ if your total taxable interest income is over $400. If you received tax-exempt interest, such as interest on municipal bonds, in the space to the left of line 2, write "TEI" and show the amount of your tax-exempt interest. DO NOT include tax-exempt interest in the total entered in the boxes on line 2.

Line 4. If you checked the "Yes" box because you can be claimed as a dependent on another person's return (such as your parents'), complete the following worksheet to figure the amount to enter on line 4. For information on dependents, see page 12 of the instruction booklet.

	A. Enter the amount from line 1 on front.	A. _____
	B. Minimum amount.	B. ____500.00
Standard deduction worksheet for dependents	C. **Compare** the amounts on lines A and B above. Enter the LARGER of the two amounts here.	C. _____
	D. Maximum amount.	D. __2,540.00
	E. **Compare** the amounts on lines C and D above. Enter the SMALLER of the two amounts here and on line 4 on front.	E. _____

Line 6. Generally, you should enter 1,900 on line 6 as your personal exemption. However, if you can be claimed as a dependent on another person's return (such as your parents'), you cannot claim a personal exemption for yourself; enter 0 on line 6. If you are entitled to additional exemptions for your spouse, for your dependent children, or for other dependents, you cannot use Form 1040EZ.

Figure your tax

Line 8. Enter the amount of Federal income tax withheld. This should be shown in Box 9 of your 1987 W-2 form(s). If you had two or more employers and had total wages of over $43,800, see page 26 of the instruction booklet. If you cannot be claimed as a dependent and you want IRS to figure your tax for you, complete lines 1 through 8, sign and date your return. If you want to figure your own tax, continue with these instructions.

Line 9. Use the amount on line 7 to find your tax in the tax table on pages 32–37 of the instruction booklet. Be sure to use the column in the tax table for **single** taxpayers. Enter the amount of tax on line 9. If your tax from the tax table is zero, enter 0.

Refund or amount you owe

Line 10. If line 8 is larger than line 9, you are entitled to a refund. Subtract line 9 from line 8, and enter the result on line 10.

Line 11. If line 9 is larger than line 8, you owe more tax. Subtract line 8 from line 9, and enter the result on line 11. Attach your check or money order for the full amount. Write your social security number, daytime phone number, and "1987 Form 1040EZ" on your payment.

Sign your return

You must sign and date your return. If you pay someone to prepare your return, that person must also sign it below the space for your signature and supply the other information required by IRS. See page 29.

Mailing your return

File your return by **April 15, 1988.** Mail it to us in the addressed envelope that came with the instruction booklet. If you don't have an addressed envelope, see page 3 for the address.

Key words

calculator	exemptions	gross	computations
percentage	estimate	net	refund
withholding	file	itemize	inherited
			will

I. Use one of the key words above in the following sentences. Use each word only once.

1. _____ income is larger than _____ income.
2. He bought a new _____.
3. In our company, the sales people get a _____ of the net sales.
4. In her _____, she left her art collection to her daughter. Her son _____ the house.
5. If you over-pay your taxes, you'll get a _____.
6. My employer is _____ too much from my paycheck.
7. The consultant made an _____ that the company's revenues would decrease next year. In my estimation he's wrong.
8. After he re-checked all his _____, he discovered the error.
9. Will you _____ all your expenses, please. I need a complete list.
10. Can I _____ my tax forms late this year? I'll be out of the country on the due date.
11. She claimed three _____; one for herself and one for each of her two children.

II. Underline the correct form of the key word in parentheses.

1. How much was (withheld, withholding) from your paycheck last month?
2. Computations are done by a (compute, computer) and a calculator does (calculates, calculations).
3. Inflation has increased by 8 (percentage, per cent).
4. The officer (estimated, estimation) the value of the jewelry to be nearly a million dollars.
5. If you are not satisfied with our product, we will (refund, refunding, refunded) your money.

77

6. How many (itemize, items) do you have on your list?

7. Her secretary (mis-filing, mis-filed) the report in the wrong (file, filing).

8. We are (exemptions, exempt) from U.S. taxes because we live in Switzerland.

9. The store (gross, grossed) over $100,000 in revenues last year, but after all the expenses were paid, the owners (net, netted) only $10,000.

10. Mr. Thriftbottom wants to change his (will, wills) again because he doesn't want his youngest son to (inheritance, inherit) a penny.

III. Use the correct form of the key word in these sentences.

1. (estimate) In my _____, his _____ is much too high.

2. (item) Last year I didn't _____ my deductions.

3. (refund) This year I think I will be _____ at least $500.

4. (inherit) Before he received the money, he had to pay an _____ tax.

5. (withhold) My _____ tax will total over $10,000 this year.

6. (percentage) In my estimation, 50 _____ is too high a
   _____ to pay.
7. (calculate) This typewriter can also do _____.
8. (compute) She wants to be a _____ programmer.
9. (file) This _____ system is very confusing. I don't know
   where to _____ the marketing report.
10. (will) In his _____, he _____ everything to
    his pet cat.
11. (net) The _____ result is, we have not made a profit.
12. (gross) Your _____ income, before taxes, is lower this year.
13. (exempt) To be _____, you must have owed no federal
    income tax last year.

IV. Use one of the key words in each sentence.

1. I need a new battery for my _____.
2. The _____ of households owning two TVs has increased
   by 10% this year.
3. "Tear up my _____!" he shouted. "That rascal will
   never _____ any of my money."
4. I'm sorry Mr. Jones, but we can't give you a _____
   unless you have proof of purchase.
5. We think the government is _____ information, and we
   want the truth.
6. How many _____ are there on the agenda for today's
   meeting?
7. Because he is overweight he is _____ from military
   service.
8. Three different companys have submitted _____ for the
   cost of building the new bridge.
9. She's going to _____ a complaint against her landlord.
10. The movie *Star Wars* _____ millions of dollars at the box
    office, and _____ its producers a very nice profit.
11. According to Dr. Stargazer's _____, the new galaxy is a
    billion, million light years away.

79

Suggestions for the Teacher

These readings and the vocabulary can be used in a great variety of ways, adapted and modified as necessary, in order to fit your teaching situation. However, for your consideration, some suggestions are outlined below. In general, the readings and their accompanying exercises may be used either for self-study out of class or for group study in class.

For Self-Study. If the students are to use this book for out-of-class self-study, and if your intention is to provide at least minimal direction and control over their use of the material, it would be a good idea to orient the students to the book and how they are to use it. This can be done in the following way.

1. Go through the first reading with the students in class. See the group-study technique for one procedure. You should point out the redundant style of the readings and encourage them to get into the habit of trying to get at the meaning of a word from the context.

2. Go through the exercises with the students. Point out that there is an answer key.

For Group Study. The basic technique and the variations described below can be used for any of the passages. You can also, to vary the procedure, do some of the passages as group study and some as self-study.

1. Refer to the table of contents and have the students look at the key words for the passage. Ask them to note which ones they think they know and which ones they're not sure of or don't know.

2. Go over the list of key words for pronunciation. You can pronounce the words and simply have the students repeat them or have the students read them aloud.

3. Option A. Have the students read the entire passage silently.

   Option B. Have the students take turns reading the passage aloud. Note any pronunciation problems and correct them after everybody has read.

   Option C. You read the passage aloud while the students listen. This option can be done twice. First the students listen with their books closed; then when you read it the second time they can follow along in their books.

4. Have the students do exercises 1-4 individually. When they have finished you can ask for questions and clarify problems. As a variation, have the students do the exercises in pairs.

General Suggestions

1. Although it is best to begin with the introductory reading and proceed through the book in sequential fashion, it is not necessary to do so.

2. You can do the readings in clusters. Divide the class into three groups. Each group does a different reading and then explains its reading to the other groups, putting the key words on the board as it explains.

3. Many of the special features lend themselves to simple question and answer practice using question words: Who, When, Where, How, Why, etc. See contents on page v.

4. The special features, because they are full of facts which are not always self-explanatory, also lend themselves to student-student discussion and explanation which will heighten cultural awareness.

5. Prepare a double set of 3x5 index cards. Each key word is written on two different cards. For each reading there are usually 12 different words. Shuffle the 24 cards well and write the numbers 1 - 24 on the back. Place all the cards on the floor with only the numbers showing. Then, in turns, the students try to locate the matching pairs by calling out two numbers.

6. For review, put the key words from several readings on 3x5 index cards. Divide the class into two teams and have a contest to see which team can use the most words correctly in sentences.

ANSWERS

Introductory Exercises

I
1. luxury, necessity
2. goods, services
3. use
4. useful
5. economics, economic, economist
6. needs
7. earns

II
1. banker
2. buyer
3. seller
4. user
5. earner
6. borrower
7. economist

Money: A Short History

I
1. worth
2. precious
3. coins, bills
4. cash
5. commodity
6. currency, value
7. transaction
8. payment
9. minted
10. supply

II
1. valuable
2. supplies, commodities
3. Cashing, transaction
4. precious
5. worth
6. coinage, bills
7. currencies
8. payment
9. minted, mint

III
1. valuable, value
2. worthless
3. mint, supplied
4. commodities
5. pay, payments
6. transacted, transaction
7. cash, cashed

IV
1. bill
2. mint
3. worth, value
4. Precious
5. commodity/commodities
6. cash, payment
7. currency, currencies
8. coin, coin
9. transaction
10. supplier, supplies

Using Money

I.
1. spent, loan, borrow, lend, interest
2. exchanges, purchase, save
3. investment, gamble
4. collection, counterfeit

II
1. spend
2. lend
3. loaning
4. borrowed
5. saved, purchased
6. invests, interest
7. Gambling, gambler, collecting, collector
8. Counterfeiting
9. exchange

III
1. loaned
2. borrowed
3. interest
4. purchased
5. spent
6. counterfeiter
7. collector, collects
8. gamble, savings
9. invested
10. exchange

IV
1. collect, save, collection
2. exchange
3. counterfeiter, spend
4. invest, investment, loan
5. interest
6. gambling

Earning Money

I	II	III	IV
1. royalties	1. capitalist	1. salaries	1. employs
2. contract	2. wealthy	2. wage	2. capital
3. fee	3. contract	3. wealthy, income	3. salary
4. wages	4. income	4. consultant	4. wage
5. salary, income	5. royalty	5. employed	5. royalties
6. capital	6. wages	6. royalty	6. consultant
7. consultant	7. employees, salary	7. bonuses, raises	7. fee
8. wealthy	8. fees	8. fees	8. raise
9. employed	9. consult	9. capitalism	9. contract
10. raise	10. raises		10. income
11. bonus	11. bonuses		11. wealthy
			12. bonus

Buying and Selling

I	II	III	IV
1. retail	1. consumer	1. deal, wholesale, bargain	1. offer
2. dealer, wholesale, consumer	2. bidder	2. market, promote	2. Market
3. profit, competitors	3. dealer	3. product, compete	3. produced
4. production, distribution promotion	4. distributor	4. consumption, retailers, profits	4. competing
5. bid/offer	5. promoter	5. distributor	5. (under)-bid
6. offer/bid	6. offerer	6. offer, bid	6. profits
7. marketing	7. producer		7. consumer
8. bargain	8. wholesaler		8. dealer
	9. retailer		9. distribution
	10. competition		10. bargaining, bargain
	11. profit		11. promotion, promote, promoted

Banks

I	II	III	IV
1. deposit	1. bounce	1. reserves	1. minimum
2. withdraw	2. funds	2. deposited	2. bounce
3. reserve	3. financial	3. withdrawal	3. deposited
4. draw	4. reserve	4. balanced	4. Fund
5. statement, balance, minimum	5. balance, minimum	5. minimum	5. withdraw
6. funds	6. deposits, withdrawals	6. statement	6. draw
7. trade	7. Commerce	7. draw	7. financial
8. commercial	8. trader, draws	8. funds	8. statement
9. Financial		9. Trade	9. reserves/ reserve
10. bounced		10. financial	10. commercial
		11. commercial	11. trade
			12. bounced

Borrowing and Lending

I
1. term
2. broke
3. deed
4. owe
5. own
6. debt
7. default
8. repay
9. risk
10. credit
11. principal, mortgage
12. sum

II
1. owed, repaid
2. term, mortgage principal, payments, deed, own
3. defaulted, risk, credit
4. debtor, sum

III
1. repaid
2. owe
3. deed, deeds
4. broke
5. debts
6. (long-) term
7. mortgaged
8. owner
9. sum
10. risked
11. creditors/ creditor
12. defaulted

IV
1. owe, broke, repaid
2. mortgage, deed, own
3. (short-) term
4. debt, risked
5. sum, credit
6. defaulted, principal

Plastic Money

I
1. accept
2. rent
3. transfer
4. cost, down payment, installment
5. stolen, amount
6. charge, rating, limit
7. sales

II
1. stole
2. charge
3. accept
4. sales
5. unlimited
6. cost
7. rented
8. amounted
9. transferred
10. rating

III
1. rent
2. accepting
3. installments
4. transferred
5. cost
6. stolen
7. charge
8. Sale
9. limit
10. amount
11. payments

IV
1. transfer
2. down payment
3. accept
4. amount
5. limit
6. sales
7. stolen
8. charge
9. renting, costs, rating
10. installment

Investing

I
1. cheap, expensive
2. price, gain
3. securities, safe
4. broker, shares
5. yield
6. dividend
7. issues
8. trend

II
1. dividend
2. gainers
3. broker, trend
4. price
5. expensive
6. cheaper
7. issued, yielded
8. security
9. shares, safe

III
1. expensive, cheapest
2. (highest-) priced
3. security
4. shares
5. safest
6. broker
7. gained
8. trend
9. (re-) issue
10. Dividends
11. yield

IV
1. safe
2. broker
3. gain
4. expensive/cheap, cheap/expensive
5. price
6. trend
7. issued
8. dividend
9. share (holder)
10. Securities
11. yield

Budgeting and Accounting

I	II	III	IV
1. expense	1. deficit, revenues, deficient	1. deficit	1. forecast
2. revenue	2. fiscal	2. liabilities	2. allowance
3. deficit	3. allowance	3. allowed	3. bottom line
4. liability	4. forecaster	4. account	4. deficit
5. asset	5. expenditures	5. counting	5. Revenue
6. equity	6. accountant, accounts	6. revenues	6. fiscally, fiscal
7. bottom line	7. Assets	7. fiscally	7. assets
8. count	8. counted	8. Forecasting	8. liabilities, equity
9. entities	9. entity, (non)-entity	9. expenditures	9. count
10. allowance			10. (non)-entity
11. fiscal			11. expenses/ expenditures
12. forecast			12. account
13. account			

Insurance

I	II	III	IV
1. pension	1. pensioner	1. policies	1. policy/coverage
2. compulsory	2. beneficiary	2. beneficiaries	2. disasters
3. policy, protection	3. disabled	3. coverage	3. protect
4. disaster	4. deduction	4. compensated	4. beneficiary
5. disability	5. policy holder	5. protected	5. premium
6. beneficiary	6. covered	6. disabled	6. sue
7. premium, coverage	7. protected	7. deducting	7. pension, deducts, compulsory
8. sue	8. compensated	8. disastrous	8. disabled
9. deductible	9. sues	9. sued	9. compensated
10. compensation	10. disastrous	10. compulsory	10. coverage
	11. compulsory		
	12. premiums		

Gambling

I	II	III	IV
1. bet/wager	1. Betting	1. bet, bet	1. stakes
2. huge	2. winner	2. folded	2. odds
3. stakes	3. illegal	3. winnings	3. chance
4. odds	4. luckily	4. staked	4. pass
5. chance	5. hugest	5. (un)fortunate	5. huge
6. won	6. passed	6. legalized	6. winning
7. favorite	7. fold	7. wager	7. fortunes
8. pass	8. favorite	8. huge	8. folds
9. fortune	9. odds	9. odds	9. wager/bet
10. wagered	10. chance	10. favorite	10. lucky
11. folded	11. fortunate	11. lucky, luck	11. favorite
12. legalizing	12. staking	12. passes	12. illegally
13. unlucky	13. wager	13. chances	13. bet

Changing Money

I
1. exports, imports
2. official
3. Monetary
4. change
5. flow
6. volume
7. convert
8. denomination
9. Inflation
10. float
11. stable
12. speculate

II
1. change
2. exported, imported
3. convert
4. flow
5. officially
6. stability
7. inflationary
8. Speculation
9. floating
10. monetary

III
1. importer, exporter
2. converted
3. change
4. denomination
5. official, officially, official
6. stability
7. monetary
8. Inflation
9. floated/floating, floating
10. Speculators
11. flow, volume

IV
1. change
2. converted, speculation
3. exported, imports
4. official
5. inflation
6. monetary
7. denominations
8. stable
9. floating
10. volume
11. flowing

Death and Taxes

I
1. Gross, net
2. calculator
3. percentage
4. will, inherited
5. refund
6. withholding
7. estimate
8. computations
9. itemize
10. file
11. exemptions

II
1. withheld
2. computer, calculations
3. per cent
4. estimated
5. refund
6. items
7. mis-filed, file
8. exempt
9. grossed, netted
10. will, inherit

III
1. estimation, estimate
2. itemize
3. refunded
4. inheritance
5. withholding
6. per cent, percentage
7. calculations/ calculation
8. computer
9. filing, file
10. will, willed
11. net
12. gross
13. exempt

IV
1. calculator
2. percentage
3. will, inherit
4. refund
5. withholding
6. items
7. exempt
8. estimates
9. file
10. grossed, netted
11. computations

Key Word Index

Sources and Resources

Bernstein, Peter L., **A Primer on Money, Banking and Gold,** Randon House, New York: 1968.

Clarke, William L., and George Pulay, **The World's Money: How It Works,** Praeger, New York: 1970.

Collier's Encyclopedia, Macmillan Publishers, New York: 1985.

Dunn, Philip, **The Book of Money Lists,** Arrow Books, London: 1985.

Galbraith, John Kenneth, **Money: Whence It Came, Where It Went,** Houghton Mifflin Co., Boston: 1975.

New Encyclopædia Britannica, 15th Edition, Encylclopædia Britannica, Inc., Chicago: 1982.

World Book Encyclopedia, World Book, Inc., Chicago: 1984.

Other Vocabureaders from Pro Lingua Associates

American Holidays: Exploring Traditions, Customs and Backgrounds. Barbara Klebanow and Sara Fischer, 1986.

Potluck: Exploring American Foods and Meals. Raymond C. Clark, 1985.

Summer Olympic Games: Exploring International Athletic Competition. Raymond C. Clark and Michael Jerald. 1987.

The Zodiac: Exploring Human Qualities and Characteristics. Mary R. Moore, 1984.

Resource Handbooks for Language Teachers:

Language Teaching Techniques, 2nd, Revised Edition. Raymond C. Clark, 1987.

The ESL Miscellany. Raymond C. Clark, Patrick R. Moran and Arthur A. Burrows. 1982.

Technology Assisted Teaching Techniques, Duncan, Janie, 1987.

Experiential Language Teaching Techniques, 2nd, Revised Edition. Michael Jerald and Raymond C. Clark, 1988.

Cultural Awareness Teaching Techniques, Jan Gaston, 1983.